New Directions for
Student Services

Elizabeth J. Whitt
EDITOR-I

John H. ....
ASSOCIATE EDITOR

D0779832

Preventing College Student Suicide

Deborah J. Taub
Jason Robertson
EDITORS

Number 141 • Spring 2013
Jossey-Bass
San Francisco

362.28
P0444
2013

PREVENTING COLLEGE STUDENT SUICIDE
Deborah J. Taub and Jason Robertson (eds.)
New Directions for Student Services, no. 141

Elizabeth J. Whitt, Editor-in-Chief
John H. Schuh, Associate Editor

NEW DIRECTIONS FOR STUDENT SERVICES (ISSN 0164-7970, e-ISSN 1536-0695) is part of The Jossey-Bass Higher and Adult Education Series and is published quarterly by Wiley Subscription Services, Inc., A Wiley Company, at Jossey-Bass, One Montgomery Street, Suite 1200, San Francisco, CA 94104-4594. Periodicals Postage Paid at San Francisco, California, and at additional mailing offices. POSTMASTER: Send address changes to New Directions for Student Services, Jossey-Bass, One Montgomery Street, Suite 1200, San Francisco, CA 94104-4594.

New Directions for Student Services is indexed in CIJE: Current Index to Journals in Education (ERIC), Contents Pages in Education (T&F), Current Abstracts (EBSCO), Education Index/Abstracts (H.W. Wilson), Educational Research Abstracts Online (T&F), ERIC Database (Education Resources Information Center), and Higher Education Abstracts (Claremont Graduate University).

Microfilm copies of issues and articles are available in 16mm and 35mm, as well as microfiche in 105mm, through University Microfilms Inc., 300 North Zeeb Road, Ann Arbor, Michigan 48106-1346.

SUBSCRIPTIONS cost $89 for individuals in the U.S., Canada, and Mexico, and $113 in the rest of the world for print only; $89 in all regions for electronic only; and $98 in the U.S., Canada, and Mexico for combined print and electronic; and $122 for combined print and electronic in the rest of the world. Institutional print only subscriptions are $275 in the U.S., $315 in Canada and Mexico, and $349 in the rest of the world; electronic only subscriptions are $275 in all regions; and combined print and electronic subscriptions are $316 in the U.S., $356 in Canada and Mexico, and $390 in the rest of the world.

EDITORIAL CORRESPONDENCE should be sent to the Editor-in-Chief, Elizabeth J. Whitt, Saint Louis University, 221 N. Grand Blvd. DuBourg Hall, Rm. 455, St. Louis, MO 63103.

www.josseybass.com

CONTENTS

EDITORS' NOTES

Today's college students consistently report feeling overwhelmed and also report high levels of stress, depression, and hopelessness (American College Health Association [ACHA], 2007). Feelings of depression and hopelessness, in particular, are significant risk factors for suicide.

Among college students, suicide is the second-leading cause of death; an estimated 1,088 college students die by suicide each year (National Mental Health Association and the Jed Foundation, 2002). The rate of attempted suicide may be as high as somewhere between 100 and 200 for every completed suicide (American Association of Suicidology, 2004). According to the ACHA (2007), one in ten college students reported having seriously considered suicide in the last twelve months.

The National Strategy for Suicide Prevention (NSSP; U. S. Department of Health and Human Services Office of the Surgeon General and National Alliance for Suicide Prevention, 2012) has called for the recognition of suicide as a significant public health problem and for taking a public health approach to suicide prevention. For colleges and universities this means a comprehensive, multifaceted approach that is focused both on at-risk populations and the general population and that is not left solely to counselors and counseling centers to implement (Suicide Prevention Resource Center, 2004). Drum, Brownson, Burton Denmark, and Smith (2009) referred to this as a problem-focused (as opposed to an individual-focused) paradigm "that requires the entire campus community to share responsibility for reducing student suicidality" (p. 220).

Since 2005, 138 campuses have received funding under the Garrett Lee Smith Memorial Act to implement campus suicide prevention programs. (See www.sprc.org/grantees for more information about the grants and grantees.) These campuses have taken a variety of approaches to prevent, treat, and respond to suicide on their campuses. This sourcebook highlights successful strategies implemented by grantee campuses that can serve as models for suicide prevention on other campuses.

The first two chapters set the context for the book. Chapter One addresses the overarching landscape of college student mental health. Deborah Taub and Jalonda Thompson outline what has been called "the campus mental health crisis" (Kadison and DiGeronimo, 2004) and the need for a comprehensive approach to the complex problem of campus suicide prevention. In Chapter Two, Elizabeth Jodoin and Jason Robertson situate suicide prevention within a public health context, as called for by the NSSP. In this chapter, they present the National Mental Health Association and Jed Foundation model (2002) for suicide prevention.

The remaining five chapters address specific components of a comprehensive suicide prevention program with illustration from college campuses that have received Garrett Lee Smith grants. Chapter Three addresses gatekeeper training, an approach to early identification and referral of students at risk for suicide. Cory Wallack, Heather Servaty-Seib, and Deborah Taub provide guidance for instituting campus gatekeeper training programs, illustrated with a campus example. In Chapter Four, Julie Catanzarite and Myles Robinson examine the role of peer education in suicide prevention and describe the creation of a peer educator program focused on mental health and suicide prevention. In Chapter Five, R. Bradley Johnson, Symphony Oxendine, Deborah Taub, and Jason Robertson describe the nature of suicide among lesbian, gay, bisexual, and transgender (LGBT) students and prevention efforts for this community. Chapter Six explores the complex nature of suicide prevention within diverse communities and populations. Richard Shadick and Sarah Akhter describe the approach they took at Pace University, New York City campus. Finally, Dolores Cimini and Estela Rivero highlight the important role that postsuicide intervention—what you do after a tragedy—plays in campus suicide prevention efforts in Chapter Seven.

An important note about the evaluation of effectiveness of comprehensive suicide prevention efforts: suicide is a low-incidence event, that is, the number of suicides, or even suicide attempts, on a single campus in any given year is likely to be relatively small (Haas, Hendin, and Mann, 2003; Silverman, 1993). Therefore, it is not effective to attempt to evaluate prevention efforts using the number of suicides or suicide attempts on campus (Schwartz and Reifler, 1988). Instead, those working in suicide prevention have measured related variables including numbers of referrals to counseling and levels of knowledge and awareness about campus resources and suicide warning signs to evaluate the effectiveness of their efforts.

Suicide is a preventable cause of death (National Institute of Mental Health, 2010); former U.S. Surgeon General David Satcher identified it as the most preventable (U. S. Department of Health and Human Services Office of the Surgeon General and National Alliance for Suicide Prevention, 2012). Students who receive counseling are six times less likely to take their own lives (Schwartz, 2006) than those who do not receive counseling. The approaches outlined in this volume represent elements of an effective comprehensive approach to campus suicide prevention.

Deborah J. Taub
Jason Robertson
Editors

References

American Association of Suicidology. *Youth Fact Sheet*, 2004. Retrieved December 5, 2011, from www.suicidology.org

American College Health Association. *American College Health Association—National College Health Assessment: Reference Group Executive Summary, Fall 2006.* Baltimore: Author, 2007.

Drum, D. J., Brownson, C., Burton Denmark, A., and Smith, S. E. "New Data on the Nature of Suicidal Crises in College Students: Shifting the Paradigm." *Professional Psychology: Research and Practice,* 2009, *40,* 213–222.

Haas, A. P., Hendin, H., and Mann, J. J. "Suicide in College Students." *American Behavioral Scientist,* 2003, *46,* 1224–1240.

Kadison, R. D., and DiGeronimo, T. F. *College of the Overwhelmed: The Campus Mental Health Crisis and What To Do About It.* San Francisco: Jossey-Bass, 2004.

National Institute of Mental Health. *Suicide: A Major, Preventable Mental Health Problem: Facts about Suicide and Suicide Prevention among Teens and Young Adults,* 2010. Downloadable fact sheet. Retrieved October 8, 2012, from www.nimh.nih.gov/health /publications/suicide-a-major-preventable-mental-health-problem-fact-sheet/suicide -a-major-preventable-mental-health-problem.shtml

National Mental Health Association and the Jed Foundation. *Safeguarding Your Students Against Suicide: Expanding the Safety Network.* Alexandria, Va.: National Mental Health Association and the Jed Foundation, 2002.

Schwartz, A. "College Student Suicide in the United States: 1990–1991 through 2003." *Journal of American College Health,* 2006, *54,* 341–352.

Schwartz, A. J., and Reifler, C. B. "College Student Suicide in the United States: Incidence Data and Prospects for Demonstrating the Efficacy of Preventative Programs." *Journal of American College Health,* 1988, 37(2), 53–59.

Silverman, M. M. "Campus Suicide Rates: Fact or Artifact?" *Suicide and Life-Threatening Behavior,* 1993, *23,* 329–342.

Suicide Prevention Resource Center. (2004). *Promoting Mental Health and Preventing Suicide in College and University Settings.* Newton, Mass.: Education Development Center.

U.S. Department of Health and Human Services Office of the Surgeon General and National Alliance for Suicide Prevention. *2001 National Strategy for Suicide Prevention: Goals and Objectives for Action.* Washington, D.C.: U.S. Department of Health and Human Services, September 2012.

U.S. Department of Health and Human Services Office of the Surgeon General and National Alliance for Suicide Prevention. *2012 National Strategy for Suicide Prevention: Goals and Objectives for Action.* Washington, D.C.: U.S. Department of Health and Human Services, September 2012.

DEBORAH J. TAUB *is professor of higher education and coordinator of the Student Personnel Administration in Higher Education program at the University of North Carolina at Greensboro. She was project director for Purdue University's Garrett Lee Smith Grant and the project evaluator for UNCG's Garrett Lee Smith Grant.*

JASON ROBERTSON *is an assistant professor at Averett University. Prior to this, he was the wellness coordinator for the Wellness Center at UNCG and served as the director of outreach and training on UNCG's SAMHSA Garret Lee Smith Grant.*

1

Suicide is the second-leading cause of death among college students. College student suicide and suicide prevention are best understood within the larger context of contemporary concerns about college student mental health.

College Student Suicide

Deborah J. Taub, Jalonda Thompson

Suicide is the second-leading cause of death among college students, and it is estimated that 1,088 college students die by suicide each year (National Mental Health Association and the Jed Foundation, 2002). Estimates are that the rate of attempted suicide is somewhere between 100 and 200 for every completed suicide (American Association of Suicidology, 2004). According to the American College Health Association (ACHA; 2007), one in ten college students reported having seriously considered suicide in the previous twelve months. The Suicide Prevention Resource Center (SPRC; 2004) has called college suicide and attempted suicide only "the tip of the iceberg of a larger mental health and substance abuse problem among college students" (p. 5).

This chapter presents the context of college student mental health within which the problem of college student suicide is situated. Because it is estimated that 90 to 95 percent of those who die by suicide have some form of treatable mental disorder at the time of their deaths, frequently depression or substance abuse (Joiner, 2010; Moscicki, 2001), the state of college student mental health today is highly relevant to campus suicide prevention. Many campus suicide prevention efforts focus on the identification of students struggling with mental health concerns and the referral of those students to counseling resources available to them before their treatable problems reach the acute stage of suicide.

This chapter was developed, in part, under grant number SMO58453-02 from SAMHSA. The views, opinions, and content of this publication are those of the authors and contributors, and do not necessarily reflect the views, opinions, or policies of CMHS, SAMHSA, or HHS, and should not be construed as such.

This chapter presents highlights of the data on college student mental health and suicide risk and protective factors. Next, we explore college students' use of counseling services and patterns of help seeking among college students. Finally, the need for a comprehensive approach to campus suicide prevention is addressed.

College students at risk for suicide can be divided into two large groups: those who come to college with an already diagnosed mental health problem and those who develop mental health problems while in college (National Mental Health Association and the Jed Foundation, 2002). Many major psychiatric illnesses, including depression, bipolar disorder, and schizophrenia, often do not manifest themselves until the late teens or early twenties (Kessler and others, 2007). The Suicide Prevention Resource Center (2004) has speculated that leaving home and going to college "may exacerbate existing psychological difficulties or trigger new ones" (p. 9). Poor sleep habits or experimentation with or abuse of drugs and alcohol, combined with the academic and social stresses of college, may play a role in triggering or worsening mental health problems in college students.

What is the extent of the "campus mental health crisis" (Kadison and DiGeronimo, 2004)? In fall 2011, the ACHA conducted the National College Health Assessment. According to the results of the study, during the previous year, 86.1 percent of respondents reported they felt overwhelmed by all they had to do, 60.5 percent felt very sad, 57.2 percent felt very lonely, 49.9 percent felt overwhelming anxiety, 45.2 percent felt that things were hopeless, and 30.3 percent felt so depressed that it was difficult to function; 6.6 percent reported they had seriously considered suicide (American College Health Association, 2012).

The Healthy Minds Study of college student mental health found that 17 percent of students screened positive for depression (Hunt and Eisenberg, 2010). College counseling centers report increased demand for services (Kitzrow, 2003) and increasing number of students with severe psychological problems (Barr, Rando, Krylowicz, and Reetz, 2010; Benton and others, 2003).

Certain groups of students are considered to be more at risk for mental health difficulties than others. Research suggests that 10 percent of college student athletes struggle with issues serious enough to warrant counseling (Ferrante, Etzel, and Lantz, 1996; Watson, 2006). Social isolation may put international students at greater risk of mental health concerns (Mori, 2000). Although women are more likely than men to have considered suicide once or twice, men are more likely to have considered suicide three or four times (National Mental Health Association and the Jed Foundation, 2002); further, men are more likely than women to complete suicide. Students under age twenty-one are more likely to exhibit suicide ideation and to attempt suicide than those over age twenty-two (National Mental Health Association and the Jed Foundation, 2002); students in the early years of college have been found to be at greatest risk (Brener, Hassan, and Barrios,

1999; Davis and DeBarros, 2006; Kisch, Leino, and Silverman, 2005). One study (Silverman and others, 1997) found graduate students to be at higher risk than undergraduates.

Westefeld, Maples, Buford, and Taylor (2001) found higher rates of suicide among gay, lesbian, and bisexual students than among heterosexual students, and Russell and Joyner (2001) found increased suicide ideation and suicide attempts in adolescents with same-sex sexual orientations. In a meta-analytic study of twenty-four studies, Marshal and colleagues (2011) found significantly higher rates of suicidality and depression among sexual minority youth than among heterosexual youth.

In addition, research has identified a number of risk factors associated with suicide (Berman, Jobes, and Silverman, 2006; Suicide Prevention Resource Center, 2011). Risk factors are variables that are associated with suicide. Risk factors for suicide (Berman, Jobes, and Silverman, 2006; Suicide Prevention Resource Center, 2011) include mental illness, alcohol and other substance abuse, hopelessness, impulsiveness and/or aggressiveness, history of trauma or abuse, previous suicide attempt, a family history of suicide, some major physical illnesses, barriers to effective care, lack of social support, stigma associated with help seeking, access to lethal means, and media that glamorizes suicide (Suicide Prevention Resource Center, 2011). The SPRC suggests that college students with one or more risk factors have a greater potential for suicidal behavior.

Protective factors are variables that "dissuade a person from considering suicide as an option" (Rutter, Freedenthal, and Osman, 2008, p. 143). Protective factors "enhance resiliency and serve to counterbalance risk factors" (Berman, Jobes, and Silverman, 2006, p. 299). These protective factors include access to effective and appropriate care, access to clinical intervention and support for help seeking, restricted access to lethal means, family and community support, cultural and religious beliefs that discourage suicide, skills in problem solving and conflict resolution, and positive beliefs about the future (Berman, Jobes, and Silverman, 2006; Suicide Prevention Resource Center, 2011; U.S. Public Health Service, 1999). Because many risk factors are difficult to change, many suicide prevention efforts have been directed at promoting protective factors.

Despite the prevalence of mental health problems among college students, students at risk of suicide often do seek the help that is available to them on campus. Although most U.S. colleges and universities provide free or low-cost counseling services for students (Gallagher, 2006; Stukenberg, Dacey, and Nagi, 2006), only a minority of those at risk seek counseling (Furr, Westefeld, McConnell, and Jenkins, 2001; Kisch, Leino, and Silverman, 2005). Nationally, an average of only slightly more than 11 percent of students sought the mental health services that were available to them (Barr, Rando, Krylowicz, and Reetz, 2010). Among college students who screened positive for depression or anxiety, between 37 percent and 84 percent, depending on the disorder, did not seek services (Eisenberg, Goldberstein, and Gollust, 2007). Nearly 50 percent of those who die by suicide in the United States had never been in contact with mental health services (Hamdi and others, 2008), and 80 to 90 percent of college students who die by suicide had not sought help from their college counseling centers (Kisch, Leino, and Silverman, 2005).

The following section looks at the groups of college students with decreased utilization of mental health services, the barriers to use of mental health services for college students, and who college students are seeking for help.

Groups With Lower Rates of Use of Mental Health Services

Colleges and universities in the United States are attempting to meet the mental health needs of a diverse student population who are coming to college "overwhelmed and more damaged than previous years" (Kitzrow, 2003, p. 169). The 2008 Chronicle of Higher Education Almanac predicted that, by 2016, the minority enrollment at colleges and universities will reach 39 percent, and 46 percent by the year 2020 (Kitzrow, 2003; Van der Werf and Sabatier, 2009.). With this increase, services offered to diverse student groups and many counselors' training are inadequate for the mental health needs of minorities, international students, students from lower socioeconomic backgrounds, and other underrepresented groups on college campuses (Kitzrow, 2003). In general, researchers suggest that students from underrepresented groups experience "higher levels of stress from social oppression and discrimination and hence have higher levels of psychological distress and, therefore, greater need for mental health services" (Rosenthal and Wilson, 2008, p. 62).

However, many of the groups with the highest need of services are the same groups seeking services at a lower rate than their counterparts (Rosenthal and Wilson, 2008). Among those who use counseling services at lower rates than risk factors might suggest are appropriate are international students (Nilsson, Berkel, Flores, and Lucas, 2004), racial and ethnic minority students (Brinson and Kottler, 1995; Davidson, Yakushka, and Sanford-Martens, 2004; Eisenberg, Golberstein, and Gollust, 2007), men (Gonzalez, Alegria, and Prihoda, 2005; Komiya, Good, and Sherrod, 2000), student athletes (Etzel, Watson, Visek, and Maniar, 2006), and graduate students (Hyun, Quinn, Madon, and Lustig, 2006).

Barriers to Utilization of Mental Health Services

Although Yorgason, Linville, and Zitzman (2008) found that students in distress were more likely to know about and use campus counseling services, they also found that there were students who were mentally distressed who "either did not know about services or knew about services but did not use them" (p. 173). Why do students not seek the help that is available? Researchers have identified several barriers to the use of mental health services by college students, including public and personal stigmas (Bathje and Pryor, 2011), lack of time (Hunt and Eisenberg, 2010; Yorgason, Linville, and Zitzman, 2008), privacy concerns, lack of emotional openness, lack of a perceived need for help, concerns about costs or insurance coverage, skepticism about treatment effectiveness (Hunt and Eisenberg, 2010), lack of knowledge of services (Yorgason, Linville, and Zitzman, 2008), and language barriers (Chu, Hsieh, and Tokars, 2011).

Who Are College Students Seeking for Assistance with Their Mental Health Needs?

In lieu of more formal sources of help, such as mental health professionals, college students seem more likely to turn to informal sources for help and support (Barksdale and Molock, 2008). Students are likely to turn to friends and family to talk about their problems (Davidson, Yakushka, and Sanford-Martens, 2004; Tiago de Melo and Farber, 2005); in one study (Oliver, Reed, Katz, and Haugh, 1999), 90 percent of students reported talking about problems to friends, and 80 percent to family.

It has long been acknowledged in higher education that the peer culture has a powerful influence on students (Chickering and Reisser, 1993; Pascarella and Terenzini, 1991, 2005). Peers are even more important to today's millennial college students (DeBard, 2004; Howe and Strauss, 2003). Researchers found that 80 percent of college students planned to seek guidance or advice from a peer in times of distress (Sharkin, Plageman, and Mangold, 2003). In the 2008 spring report, the National College Health Assessment reported 61.1 percent of the students surveyed sought information from their friends on a regular basis (American College Health Association, 2009). In another study, two-thirds of college students with suicidal thoughts who chose to tell someone told a peer (Drum, Brownson, Burton Denmark, and Smith, 2009). Research (Davidson, Yakushka, and Sanford-Martens, 2004) has found that the most frequent source of referrals to counseling for minority students who sought counseling center services came from friends.

In addition to seeking help from their peers, students say that they would turn to family to talk about their problems (Davidson, Yakushka, and Sanford-Martens, 2004; Oliver, Reed, Katz, and Haugh, 1999; Tiago de Melo and Farber, 2004). The current generation of college students is extremely close with their parents (Howe and Strauss, 2003). A recent study found that first-year college students communicated with their parents an average of 10.41 times per week, with most of that communication being initiated by parents (Grace, 2006). According to a recent Pew Research Center report (Kohut and others, 2007), approximately 80 percent of eighteen- to twenty-five-year-olds said that they had talked to their parents in the past day. Levine and Dean (2012) found that 19 percent of undergraduates are in contact with their parents three or more times daily. The parents of today's college students are close with their college-age children and actively involved in their college experience (Coburn, 2006; College Parents of America, 2007a, 2007b; Daniel, Evans, and Scott, 2001; Howe and Strauss, 2003; Levine and Dean, 2012). This closeness and active involvement has led to the term *helicopter parents*. Helicopter parents are parents or guardians who are "very overprotective and overly involved in the affairs of their children, hovering over them, and swooping down in their time of crisis" (Pricer, 2008, p. 94). However, parents can serve as an important source of support for students (Kadison and DiGeronimo, 2004; Taub, 2008) and as important allies in suicide prevention. Trela (2008) shifts the role of parents from helicopter parents to potential members of the front line who can be a valuable resource to their sons or daughters as well as the college or university as it relates to suicide prevention.

The Need for a Comprehensive Approach

Because of the tendency of so many at-risk students to underutilize counseling services and because of the complex nature of the problem of suicide, counselors and counseling centers alone cannot carry the burden of campus suicide prevention. Experts call for a comprehensive, systemic approach to campus suicide prevention (National Mental Health Association and the Jed Foundation, 2002). As stated previously, according to the Suicide Prevention Resource Center (2004), a comprehensive campus suicide prevention program should address both the general campus population and at-risk groups and will be most effective when it "includes consistent and coordinated activities in all the social spheres in which [college students] live, work, and play" (p. 16). Members of the campus community—faculty, student affairs professionals, student leaders, peer helpers, counselors, medical providers, clergy, support staff, and others—all have a role to play in such a comprehensive approach.

The National Mental Health Association and the Jed Foundation (2002) have identified seven components of a comprehensive approach to suicide prevention on college campuses: (1) identify students at risk, (2) increase help-seeking behavior, (3) provide mental health services, (4) follow crisis management procedures, (5) restrict access to potentially lethal means, (6) develop life skills, and (7) promote social networks. This approach seeks to reduce risk factors and promote protective factors (Knox and others, 2003). This comprehensive approach is described in more detail in Chapter 2.

The Suicide Prevention Resource Center (2004) suggests the formation of a diverse group of campus and off-campus partners, such as parents, to serve as the central operating structure for campus suicide prevention efforts. This group could work to integrate suicide prevention into already existing campus endeavors in substance abuse, first-year programming, health services, student activities, and so on, and to develop and coordinate new suicide prevention efforts. Exact activities and approaches will differ based on various campus contexts (student population, location, current level of services, resources, and the like). The SPRC also emphasizes the importance of campus leadership in a successful approach to campus suicide prevention.

For colleges and universities this means a comprehensive, multifaceted approach that is focused both on at-risk populations and at the general population and that is not left solely to counselors and counseling centers to implement (Suicide Prevention Resource Center, 2004). All parts of the higher education institution need to be involved and to work together to provide an effective response. As stated previously, according to the SPRC, a comprehensive campus suicide prevention program should address both the general campus population and at-risk groups and will be most effective when it "includes consistent and coordinated activities in all the social spheres in which [college students] live, work, and play" (Suicide Prevention Resource Center, 2004, p. 16). This approach calls on all areas of the campus to work together to create a suicide prevention safety net.

References

American Association of Suicidology. *Youth Fact Sheet*, 2004. Retrieved December 5, 2011, from www.suicidology.org

American College Health Association. *American College Health Association—National College Health Assessment: Reference Group Executive Summary, Fall 2006*. Baltimore: Author, 2007.

American College Health Association. "American College Health Association—National College Health Assessment Spring 2008 Reference Group Data Report (Abridged): The American College Health Association." *Journal of American College Health*, 2009, *57*, 477–488.

American College Health Association. *American College Health Association—National College Health Assessment II: Fall 2011 Reference Group Executive Summary*. Baltimore: American College Health Association, 2012.

Barksdale, C. L., and Molock, S. D. "Perceived Norms and Mental Help Seeking Among African American College Students." *Journal of Behavioral Health Services & Research*, 2008, *36*(3), 285–299.

Barr, V., Rando, R., Krylowicz, B., and Reetz, D. *The Association for University and College Counseling Center Directors Annual Survey*, 2010. Retrieved December 5, 2011, from http://aucccd.org/img/pdfs/aucccd_directors_survey_monograph_2010.pdf

Bathje, G. J., and Pryor, J. B. "The Relationships of Public and Self-Stigma to Seeking Mental Health Services." *Journal of Mental Health Counseling*, 2011, *33*(2), 161–176.

Benton, S. A., and others. "Changes in Counseling Center Client Problems Across 13 Years." *Professional Psychology: Research and Practice*, 2003, *34*, 66–72.

Berman, A. L., Jobes, D. A., and Silverman, M. M. *Adolescent Suicide: Assessment and Intervention*. (2nd ed.) Washington, D.C.: American Psychological Association, 2006.

Brener, N. D., Hassan, S. S., and Barrios, L. C. "Suicidal Ideation Among College Students in the United States." *Journal of Consulting and Clinical Psychology*, 1999, *67*, 1004–1008.

Brinson, J. A., and Kottler, J. A. "Minorities' Underutilization of Counseling Centers' Mental Health Services: A Case for Outreach and Consultation." *Journal of Mental Health Counseling,* 1995, *17,* 371–385.

Chickering, A. W., and Reisser, L. *Education and Identity.* (2nd ed.) San Francisco: Jossey-Bass, 1993.

Chu, J. P., Hsieh, K.-Y., and Tokars, D. A. "Help-Seeking Tendencies in Asian Americans with Suicidal Ideation and Attempts." *Asian American Journal of Psychology,* 2011, *2,* 25–38.

Coburn, K. L. "Organizing a Ground Crew for Today's Helicopter Parents." *About Campus,* July/Aug. 2006, pp. 9–16.

College Parents of America. "Second Annual National Survey on College Parent Experiences." 2007a. Retrieved May 21, 2007, from www.collegeparents.org/files/2007-Current-Parent-Survey-Summary.pdf

College Parents of America. "Second Annual National Survey on Future College Parent Expectations." 2007b. Retrieved May 21, 2007, from www.collegeparents.org/files/2007-Future-Parent-Survey.pdf

Daniel, B. V., Evans, S. G., and Scott, B. R. "Understanding Family Involvement in the College Experience Today." In B. V. Daniel and B. R. Scott (eds.), *Consumers, Adversaries, and Partners: Working With the Families of Undergraduates.* San Francisco: Jossey-Bass, 2001.

Davidson, M. M., Yakushka, O. F., and Sanford-Martens, T. C. "Racial and Ethnic Minority Clients' Utilization of a University Counseling Center: An Archival Study." *Journal of Multicultural Counseling and Development,* 2004, *32,* 259–271.

Davis, R., and DeBarros, A. "In College, First Year Is by Far the Riskiest." *USA Today,* Jan. 25, 2006. Retrieved December 6, 2011, from www.usatoday.com/news/nation/2006-01-24-campus-deaths-cover_x.htm#

DeBard, R. "Millennials Coming to College." In M. D. Coomes and R. DeBard (eds.), *Serving the Millennial Generation.* New Directions for Student Services, no. 106. San Francisco: Jossey-Bass, 2004.

Drum, D. J., Brownson, C., Burton Denmark, A., and Smith, S. E. "New Data on the Nature of Suicidal Crises in College Students: Shifting the Paradigm." *Professional Psychology: Research and Practice,* 2009, *40,* 213–222.

Eisenberg, D., Golberstein, E., and Gollust, S. E. "Help-Seeking and Access to Mental Health Care in a University Student Population." *Medical Care,* 2007, *45,* 594–601.

Etzel, E. F., Watson, J. C., Visek, A. J., and Maniar, S. D. "Understanding and Promoting College Student-Athlete Health: Essential Issues for Student Affairs Professionals." *NAPSA Journal,* 2006, *43,* 518–546.

Ferrante, A. P., Etzel, E. F., and Lantz, C. "Counseling College Student-Athletes: The Problem, the Need." In E. F. Etzel, E. P. Ferrante, and J. W. Pinkney (eds.), *Counseling College Student-Athletes: Issues and Interventions.* (2nd ed.) Morgantown, WV: Fitness Information Technology, 1996.

Furr, S. R., Westefeld, J. S., McConnell, G. N., and Jenkins, J. M. "Suicide and Depression Among College Students: A Decade Later." *Professional Psychology: Research and Practice,* 2001, *32,* 97–100.

Gallagher, R. P. *National Survey of Counseling Center Directors.* Alexandria, Va.: International Association of Counseling Services, 2006.

Gonzalez, J. M., Alegria M., and Prihoda, T. J. "How Do Attitudes Toward Mental Health Treatment Vary by Age, Gender, and Ethnicity/Race in Young Adults?" *Journal of Community Psychology,* 2005, *33,* 611–629.

Grace, C. O. "Family Ties." *Middlebury Magazine,* Fall 2006. Retrieved March 12, 2008, from www.middlebury.edu/administration/middmag/archive/2006/fall/features/family_ties/

Hamdi, E., and others. "Suicides Not in Contact with Mental Health Services: Risk Indicators and Determinants of Referral." *Journal of Mental Health,* 2008, *17,* 398–409.

Howe, N., and Strauss, W. *Millennials Go to College*. Great Falls, Va.: American Association of Registrars and Admissions Officers and LifeCourse Associates, 2003.

Hunt, J., and Eisenberg, D. "Mental Health Problems and Help-Seeking Behavior Among College Students." *Journal of Adolescent Health*, 2010, 4(1), 3–10.

Hyun, J. K., Quinn, B. C., Madon, T., and Lustig, S. "Graduate Student Mental Health Needs: Needs Assessment and Utilization of Counseling Services." *Journal of College Student Development*, 2006, 47, 247–266.

Joiner, T. *Myths about Suicide*. Cambridge, MA: Harvard University Press, 2010.

Kadison, R. D., and DiGeronimo, T. F. *College of the Overwhelmed: The Campus Mental Health Crisis and What To Do About It*. San Francisco: Jossey-Bass, 2004.

Kessler, R. C., and others. "Age of Onset of Mental Disorders: A Review of Recent Literature." *Current Opinion in Psychiatry*, 2007, 20, 359–364.

Kisch, J., Leino, E. V., and Silverman, M. M. "Aspects of Suicidal Behavior, Depression, and Treatment in College Students: Results from the Spring 2000 National College Health Assessment Survey." *Suicide and Life-Threatening Behavior*, 2005, 35, 3–13.

Kitzrow, M. A. "The Mental Health Needs of Today's College Students: Challenges and Recommendations." *NASPA Journal*, 2003, 41, 165–179.

Knox, K. L., and others. "Risk of Suicide and Related Adverse Outcomes after Exposure to a Suicide Prevention Program in the U.S. Air Force: Cohort Study." *British Medical Journal*, 2003, 327, 1376–1378.

Kohut, A., and others. *How Young People View Their Lives, Futures, and Politics: A Portrait of "Generation Next."* Washington, D.C.: Pew Research Center for the People and the Press, 2007. Retrieved May 21, 2007, from http://people-press.org/reports/display.php3?ReportID=300

Komiya, N., Good, G. E., and Sherrod, N. B. "Emotional Openness as a Predictor of College Students' Attitudes Toward Seeking Professional Psychological Help." *Journal of Counseling Psychology*, 2000, 47, 138–143.

Levine, A., and Dean, D. R. *Generation on a Tightrope*. San Francisco: Jossey-Bass, 2012.

Marshal, M. P., and others. "Suicidality and Depression Disparities Between Sexual Minority and Heterosexual Youth: A Meta-analytic Review." *Journal of Adolescent Health*, 2011, 49, 115–123.

Mori, S. C. "Addressing the Mental Health Concerns of International Students." *Journal of Counseling and Development*, 2000, 78, 137–144.

Moscicki, E. K. "Epidemiology of Completed and Attempted Suicide: Toward a Framework for Prevention." *Clinical Neuroscience Research*, 2001, 1, 310–323.

National Mental Health Association and the Jed Foundation. *Safeguarding Your Students Against Suicide: Expanding the Safety Network*. Alexandria, Va.: National Mental Health Association and the Jed Foundation, 2002.

Nilsson, J. E., Berkel, L. A., Flores, L. Y., and Lucas, M. S. "Utilization Rate and Presenting Concerns of International Students at a University Counseling Center: Implications for Outreach Programming." *Journal of College Student Psychotherapy*, 2004, 19(2), 49–59.

Oliver, J. M., Reed, C.K.S., Katz, B. M., and Haugh, J. A. "Students' Self-Reports of Help-Seeking: The Impact of Psychological Problems, Stress, and Demographic Variables on Utilization of Formal and Informal Support." *Social Behavior and Personality*, 1999, 27, 109–128.

Pascarella, E. T., and Terenzini, P. T. *How College Affects Students: Findings and Insights from Twenty Years of Research*. San Francisco: Jossey-Bass, 1991.

Pascarella, E. T., and Terenzini, P. T. *How College Affects Students: A Third Decade of Research*, vol. 2. San Francisco: Jossey-Bass, 2005.

Pricer, W. F. "At Issue: Helicopter Parents and Millennial Students, an Annotated Bibliography." *Community College Enterprise*, 2008, 93–108.

Rosenthal, B., and Wilson, C. "Mental Health Services: Use and Disparity Among Diverse College Students." *Journal of American College Health*, 2008, 57, 61–67.

Russell, S. T., and Joyner, K. "Adolescent Sexual Orientation and Suicide Risk: Evidence from a National Study." *American Journal of Public Health,* 2001, *91,* 1276–1281.

Rutter, P. A., Freedenthal, S., and Osman, A. "Assessing Protection from Suicidal Risk: Psychometric Properties of the Suicide Resilience Inventory." *Death Studies,* 2008, *32,* 142–153.

Sharkin, B. S., Plageman, P. M., and Mangold, S. L. "College Student Response to Peers in Distress: An Exploratory Study." *Journal of College Student Development,* 2003, *44,* 691–698.

Silverman, M. M., and others. "The Big Ten Student Suicide Study: A 10-Year Study of Suicides on Midwestern University Campuses." *Suicide and Life Threatening Behavior,* 1997, *27,* 285–303.

Stukenberg, K. W., Dacey, C. M., and Nagi, M. S. "Psychotherapy Services Provided by a College Counseling Center: Continuity Through Change Over 37 Years." *Journal of College Student Psychotherapy Journal,* 2006, *20,* 53–70.

Suicide Prevention Resource Center. *Promoting Mental Health and Preventing Suicide in College and University Settings.* Newton, Mass.: Education Development Center, 2004.

Suicide Prevention Resource Center, and Rogers, P. "Understanding Risk and Protective Factors forSuicide: A Primer for Preventing Suicide," 2011. Retrieved December 19, 2012, from www.sprc.org/sites/sprc.org/files/library/RandPPrimer.pdf

Taub, D. J. "The Impact of Parents on Student Development." In K. Carney (ed.), *Managing Parent Partnerships: Maximizing Influence, Minimizing Interference, and Focusing on Student Success.* New Directions for Student Services, no. 122. San Francisco: Jossey-Bass, 2008.

Tiago de Melo, J. A., and Farber, B. A. "Willingness to Seek Help for Psychosocial Problems Among Latino and White American College Students." *Psychological Reports,* 2005, *97,* 50–52.

Trela, K. Facing mental health crises on campus. *About Campus,* 2008, *12,* 30–32.

U.S. Public Health Service. *The Surgeon General's Call to Action to Prevent Suicide.* Washington, D.C.: U.S. Public Health Service/Department of Health and Human Services, 1999.

Van der Werf, M., and Sabatier, G. *The College of 2020: Students.* Washington, D.C.: Chronicle Research Services, Chronicle of Higher Education, 2009.

Watson, J. C. "Student-Athletes and Counseling: Factors Influencing the Decision to Seek Counseling Services." *College Student Journal,* 2006, *40,* 35–42.

Westefeld, J., Maples, M., Buford, B., and Taylor, S. "Gay, Lesbian and Bisexual College Students: The Relationship Between Sexual Orientation and Depression, Loneliness and Suicide." *Journal of College Student Psychotherapy,* 2001, *15,* 71–82.

Yorgason, J., Linville, D., and Zitzman, B. "Mental Health Among College Students: Do Those Who Need Services Know About and Use Them?" *Journal of American College Health,* 2008, *57*(2), 173–181.

DEBORAH J. TAUB *is professor of higher education and coordinator of the Student Personnel Administration in Higher Education program at the University of North Carolina at Greensboro.*

JALONDA THOMPSON *is coordinator of exploratory advising at the University of North Carolina at Greensboro.*

NEW DIRECTIONS FOR STUDENT SERVICES • DOI: 10.1002/ss

This chapter explores public health theories and approaches to suicide prevention on campus. Implications for student affairs and higher education personnel regarding suicide prevention programming are discussed.

The Public Health Approach to Campus Suicide Prevention

Elizabeth C. Jodoin, Jason Robertson

The perception that college students are coming to campus with more severe psychological concerns than in the past has been empirically supported on college campuses (Benton and others, 2003). Approximately 20 percent of all adolescents have a diagnosable mental health disorder (Kessler and others, 2005), many of which then continue on to college and take their mental health issues with them. Mowbray and others (2006) report that 12 to 18 percent of college students manifest a diagnosable psychiatric condition. Due to the many interpersonal and institutional influences and factors associated with mental health concerns while attending college (Byrd and McKinney, 2012), suicide prevention, as discussed in Chapter One, requires interventions above and beyond traditional treatment and medical models. Interventions are required that take a holistic and comprehensive approach to addressing the concerns not only for individuals, but also at the community and organizational levels.

This chapter focuses first on the impact of college and the campus ecology (that is, built environment, policies, community, and so on) on student mental health. Next, comprehensive public health models to address suicide prevention are reviewed. Finally, planning models related to public health and campus suicide prevention and implications for effective practice are discussed.

In 1999, the U.S. surgeon general declared that suicide was a major public health concern (U.S. Public Health Service, 1999). Public health may be defined as community efforts that are implemented not only to improve one's personal health, but to create policies and programs to initiate and maintain one's health in society (Schneider, 2011). The public health approach strives to capture not only the high-risk individuals who might not be seeking individual treatment, but also the general population in a global preventative effort, thereby meeting individuals at their present level of functioning (Davidson and Locke, 2010; Potter, Powell, and Kachur, 1995).

Given public health's potential to influence mental health concerns and, in turn, suicide through early intervention, the National Strategy for Suicide Prevention, the Jed Foundation, and the Suicide Prevention Resource Center (SPRC) have endorsed the public health approach as the most effective approach to address this monumental public health concern (National Mental Health Association and the Jed Foundation, 2002; Suicide Prevention Resource Center, 2002, 2004; Jed Foundation and Education Development Center, 2011; U.S Department of Health and Human Services Office of the Surgeon General and National Action Alliance for Suicide Prevention, 2012).

The Impact of College and Campus Ecology on Student Mental Health

Higher education presents many challenges for students who are struggling with a mental health concern. These challenges include academic functioning, persistence (Martin, 2010; Megivern, Pellerito, and Mowbray, 2003), and interpersonal relationships (Parrish and Tunkle, 2005).

The experience of suicidal ideation in undergraduate students may be influenced by a sense of belonging, or lack thereof, on campus (Van Orden and others, 2008). Students might perceive the campus environment as being alienating and isolating (Curtis, 2010). Thus, the college community and institutional characteristics strongly affect the experience of suicidal ideation and mental health concerns (Byrd and McKinney, 2012; Siggins, 2010; Van Orden and others, 2008). Public health seeks to influence the campus ecology related to mental health concerns and suicide through multifaceted, multidisciplinary approaches to the challenges listed above.

Public Health

Winslow (1920) defined public health as "the science and the art of preventing disease, prolonging life, and promoting physical health and efficiency through organized community efforts" (p. 30). The World Health Organization (1948) defined health as "a state of complete physical, mental and social well-being and not merely the absence of disease or infirmity" (p. 100). This definition views health in a holistic manner, as it encompasses emotional health and social factors, in addition to medical concerns.

It is important to note that public health focuses primarily on the public or a community (that is, college students) as a population, rather than looking solely at individual health (McLeroy, Bibeau, Steckler, and Glanz, 1988). The public health model of mental health concerns is a departure from medical-based models of psychiatric and therapeutic care. Although one may think of mental health treatment as highly individualistic and focusing solely on the presenting concern (Rihmer, Belso, and Kiss, 2002), the primary goals of the public health approach to campus suicide prevention are to preclude mental health concerns and to endorse emotional wellness in the general college population (Davidson and Locke, 2010).

Public health refers not only to improving one's personal health, but also includes the practices and programs that are implemented to initiate and maintain one's health in society. The three core functions of public health are (1) assessment of societal health concerns and the availability of existing services, (2) policy development and enforcement of laws to safeguard health and personal safety, and (3) assurance of program quality and accessibility to the public (Schneider, 2011).

Perspectives on Public Health

Individual Perspectives. Health promotion is the joining of wellness education and environmental collaboration, in an effort to support behaviors and physical surroundings advantageous to health (Green and Kreuter, 1991; Potter, Powell, and Kachur, 1995). Although this entails individuals making sound decisions regarding their health, health promotion also requires communities to implement policies and programs to make the healthy choices and options easier for individuals to access (Davidson and Locke, 2010; Green and Kreuter, 1991; National Cancer Institute, 2005). The blending of both ecological and instructional aspects of health creates an environment that promotes individual health.

The term *health education* is closely related to health promotion. Health education not only is focused on traditional instruction related to disease prevention and treatment, but also addresses the impact of the media, community policies and environmental endeavors, and resulting influences on behavioral change (Green and Kreuter, 1991). Despite the fact that an individual may be highly motivated to change an unhealthy behavior within a specific time frame, if environmental barriers are not considered and addressed, the chance of success for sustained individual behavior change decreases (Schneider, 2011).

Ecological Perspectives. The social ecological model of public health is considered a community-level theory, as it seeks to initiate individual change by enacting institutional, community, and public policy transformations (Hayden, 2009). This theory incorporates not only education but environmental contexts in which behavioral decisions, such as suicidal ideation or actions, are made. As noted earlier, individuals at greatest risk may be missed by interventions that solely address personal health and behavioral choices and negate the value and sway of social supports and environmental influences and pressures (McLeroy, Bibeau, Steckler, and Glanz, 1988; Stokols, 1996).

The social ecological theory states that an individual's actions are affected by and in turn affect his or her social surroundings (McLeroy, Bibeau, Steckler, and Glanz, 1988). The five aspects of behavioral persuasion of the social ecological model are intrapersonal, interpersonal, institutional, community, and public policy/societal factors (see Table 2.1). These social networks may support or deter detrimental personal health actions, encourage or discourage help-seeking behavior, or inhibit or inspire conversations about one's current health (McLeroy, Bibeau, Steckler, and Glanz, 1988). McLeroy, Bibeau, Steckler, and Glanz (1988) stated that "organizational changes are necessary to support long term behavioral changes among individuals" (p. 362). It is important to note that higher education institutions may differ in resources regarding on-campus mental health treatment services, as well as differing insurance coverage for psychiatric medications and counseling. These organizational factors affect the course of treatment and overall mental health of students.

The differences between an organization and institution are important to understand when using an ecological model. A university, as an institution, has an internal culture of norms and socialization procedures depending on the university mission and current requests of society. Organizations within the university (such as athletic teams, residence halls, and living-learning communities) conform in various ways to these institutional norms (Kezar and Eckel, 2004). Policies, practices, and programs may be implemented at the federal, state, institutional, or organizational level. It is imperative that program planners understand the level of bureaucracy that they are attempting to target.

Models of Suicide Prevention

Public Health Approach to Suicide Prevention. The public health approach to suicide prevention "is widely regarded as the approach that is mostly likely to produce significant and sustained reductions in suicide" (Suicide Prevention Resource Center, 2002, p. 1). The public health approach to suicide prevention focuses upon the complex issue of suicide from many ecological levels. It is the combination of all aspects of the student's life and campus environment that leads to an effective suicide prevention program. This approach includes five steps that may overlap with one another or evolve successively. These steps include (1) defining the problem of suicide on the target campus, (2) identifying the causes of the suicides on campus, (3) testing and developing suicide prevention programming and interventions, (4) implementing these programs, and (5) evaluating the interventions (see Table 2.2). The National Mental Health Association and the Jed Foundation (2002) note that a comprehensive and multilayered approach is needed on campus to

Table 2.1. Social Ecological Model of Suicide Prevention Within a Campus Setting

Factor	Characteristics
Intrapersonal	Personal developmental and family history of mental health and alcohol and other drug concerns, individual self-concept and degree of adaptive coping skills; culture, race, ethnicity, spiritual beliefs, sexual orientation and gender identity; personal beliefs, internalized stigma, perceptions and education about mental health concerns and supposed value of treatment; personal perceptions about self, others, campus, and world ecology; focus is on individual behavior change.
Interpersonal	Interactions and assumed roles with informal and formal social systems; the collective standards and views regarding stigma and discrimination toward individuals with mental health concerns; campus alcohol and drug cultures; influences of social media and technology; focus is on increasing social networks and supports to influence personal change.
Institutional	Institutional attributes, stated and unstated policies and rules for institutional culture and functioning, such as student health insurance policies, availability, duration and access of on-campus mental health services, psychiatric leave of absence or withdrawal policies, and the existence of behavioral threat assessment teams; campus media relations and relationship with local news outlets; access to lethal means on campus (availability of alcohol and drugs on campus, prohibition of weapons and guns on campus, lethal substances found on campus and the security of these chemicals) and environmental harm factors (scaffolding, bridges, unsecured rooftops) that may be used as a method of attempting suicide; focus is on creating organizational change that will positively affect behavior change within the individual.
Community	Networks among local institutions and organizations; availability and affordability of local mental health treatment and the institution's relationship with these settings (inpatient and outpatient settings, psychiatry services, emergency assessments, mobile treatment teams); campus peer mental health education program and relationship with community stakeholders; focus is on creating transformations in local organizations and surroundings that will positively influence the institution, which will in turn affect group and peer behavior, thereby benefiting the individual.
Public Policy/ Societal Factors	Policies, programs, and laws at the federal, state, and local levels related to mental health concerns such as health insurance coverage, laws regarding possession of lethal means, and medical and educational confidentiality laws; impact of institutional, academic, and organizational policies regarding student mental health; focus is on creating broad level changes that will influence community and institutional factors.

Sources: McLeroy, Bibeau, Steckler, and Glanz, 1988; Davidson and Locke, 2010; Hayden, 2009.

Table 2.2. The Public Health Approach to Suicide Prevention

Defining the Problem of Suicide on Campus	Identifying the rates of deaths by suicide on campus; exploring events surrounding the death; investigating the impact the death had on the campus community.
Identifying the Causes of the Death by Suicide	Identifying risk factors (what raises the probability of thoughts of suicide or suicidal behavior, such as loss of a relationship, feelings of hopelessness) and protective factors (what decreases the probability of students acting on suicidal thoughts or behaviors, such as supportive social networks, spirituality).
Developing and Testing Interventions	Interventions should address many populations such as student athletes; international students; gay, lesbian, bisexual, transgender, queer, and questioning students; and racial and ethnic minority students; the psychological and developmental stages of the target population needs to be considered as well.
Implementing Interventions	Pretests and posttests to ensure program quality and consistency and that main objectives are being met; communication is imperative between key stakeholders (program staff, student affairs personnel, and campus and community mental health providers).
Evaluating the Effectiveness of the Interventions	The program must be deemed ethical and safe for participants; the goals are quantifiable, easily assessed, and readily achieved in the desired time frame.

Source: Suicide Prevention Resource Center, 2002.

meet the needs of the complicated and multifaceted issue of suicidal ideation and behaviors.

Planning Models Applied to Public Health and Suicide Prevention. As discussed in Chapter One, suicide is the second-leading cause of death among college students. To develop a comprehensive suicide prevention program, it is necessary to develop a clear understanding of the issues confronting students on each campus. One way to understand these issues and concerns and to organize the material is through the utilization of planning models and through the use of behavior change theory to address each concern.

One model that has commonly been used in developing comprehensive suicide prevention programs is the model put forth by the Jed Foundation (see Figure 2.1). This model, developed with assistance from the SPRC, is a research-based model that allows institutions to determine potential gaps in their prevention efforts (Jed Foundation and Suicide Prevention Resource Center, n. d.). Utilizing this model, campuses can define their areas of strength and weakness. The model includes (1) increasing access to help-seeking behavior, (2) providing mental health services, (3) identifying and following crisis management protocol, (4) restricting lethal means,

Figure 2.1. Jed Foundation and SPRC Research-Based Model of Comprehensive Suicide Prevention

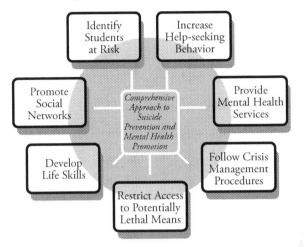

(5) developing life skills, (6) promoting social supports and networks, and (7) identifying students at risk. From an examination of this model, campuses can engage in an ecological assessment of the strengths of the campus in terms of service delivery, policy, and prevention programming.

It is important to note that this is just one model that can be applied to suicide prevention and can serve as a source of evaluation and a place to start in terms of issue identification and program development. Other models and theories have a strong place in the development of comprehensive programs. Some of these include the PRECEDE-PROCEED Model (Green, 1984) and behavior change theories such as the Health Belief Model and the Transtheoretical Model (National Cancer Institute, 2005). Using these can help to ensure that the programs developed to address suicide on the college campuses are evidence based and theory informed. These programs can then lead to efficient and efficacious change on a college campus and affect the community as a whole.

Implications for Practice

The crux of public health approaches in suicide prevention programming is on promoting wellness and the prevention of mental health concerns and suicidal ideation and behaviors in the general campus population (Davidson and Locke, 2010; Green and Kreuter, 1991). Environmental and ecological aspects of the campus and local community must be considered to create an effective suicide prevention program. Ways to assess these areas are addressed within the Jed Foundation and SPRC research-based model of comprehensive suicide prevention.

The increasing acuteness of student mental health concerns and amplified need for services may affect student affairs staff in addition to faculty, who might be on the forefront of noticing and managing students' psychological concerns (Kitzrow, 2009). A comprehensive suicide prevention program on campus includes informative programming for faculty, staff, parents and families, clergy, members of the athletic department, and resident assistants for a campus to have a successful suicide prevention initiative (National Mental Health Association and the Jed Foundation, 2002; Siggins, 2010). Keup (2008) reports that there is a need for all members of a campus community to be aware of signs of psychological distress.

Mental health services should be accessible on a university campus (Mowbray and others, 2006). Campus staff and faculty may have different levels of awareness and understanding of state and federal confidentiality laws, and this must be taken into consideration when promoting communication among colleagues (Randazzo and Plummer, 2009). However, a general deficit in student, faculty, and staff awareness of campus mental health services and resources has been noted in the literature (Becker and others, 2002; Curtis, 2010; Eisenberg, Golberstein, and Gollust, 2007; King, Vidourek, and Strader, 2008; Quinn, Wilson, MacIntyre, and Tinklin, 2009). Higher education professionals would benefit from having basic knowledge of referral procedures, and obtaining education on the symptoms of common mental health concerns, including suicidal ideation, attempts, and responding after a suicide has occurred and debriefing (Trela, 2008).

Good points of entry for suicide prevention programming may be living and learning communities, athletic teams, Greek organizations, and interest-specific groups and clubs, as these groups inherently employ numerous layers of ecological influences. Some of the ways student affairs professionals and faculty may enhance their education regarding suicide prevention and mental health concerns is by attending a suicide prevention gatekeeper training (see Chapter Three) and participating in campus peer mental health education programs (see Chapter Four). Learning more about the specific ecology and institutional norms of one's campus may prove to be highly beneficial when talking with a distressed student, view the student in the most holistic manner possible (see Table 2.3 for selected resources related to the social ecological model).

Table 2.3. Selected Suicide Prevention Resources Based on the Social Ecological Model

Intrapersonal Factors	*The Jed Foundation, www.jedfoundation.org* Videos: *Half of Us Campaign,* www.halfofus.com 　*The Suicide Prevention Resource Center,* www.sprc.org **Publication:** *Suicide Risk and Prevention for Lesbian, Gay, Bisexual, and Transgender Youth* (2008), www.sprc.org/library/SPRC_LGBT_Youth.pdf
Interpersonal Factors	*American College Health Association, www.acha.org* **Publication:** *How to Help a Friend with a Drinking Problem* (2010), http://members.acha.org/source/orders/index.cfm?section=unknown&task=1&StartRow=6&PageNum=2&SEARCH_TYPE=find&FindSpec=&continue=1&CATEGORY=BROCHURES&FindIn=
Institutional Factors	*The Substance Abuse and Mental Health Services Administration, www.samhsa.gov* **Funding:** Garrett Lee Smith Campus Suicide Prevention grants, www.samhsa.gov/grants/2011/sm_11_002.aspx *The Jed Foundation, www.jedfoundation.org* **Webinars:** Campus Mental Health Action Planning (MHAP) Webinars, www.jedfoundation.org/programs/campusMHAP-webinars
Community Factors	*The Suicide Prevention Resource Center,* www.sprc.org **Document:** Community Coalition Suicide Prevention "Checklist" (2001), www.sprc.org/library/ccspchecklist.pdf
Public Policy Factors	*American Foundation for Suicide Prevention, www.afsp.org* **Document:** 2011 Federal and State Public Policy Priorities, www.afsp.org/?fuseaction=home.download&folder_file_id=09D7CF78-E576-F47B-F109A83391BCAD1A

References

Becker, M., and others. "Students With Mental Illnesses in a University Setting: Faculty and Student Attitudes, Beliefs, Knowledge, and Experiences." *Psychiatric Rehabilitation Journal,* 2002, 25(4), 359–368.

Benton, S. A., and others. "Changes in Counseling Center Client Problems Across 13 Years." *Professional Psychology: Research and Practice,* 2003, 34(1), 66–72.

Byrd, D. R., and McKinney, K. J. "Individual, Interpersonal, and Institutional Level Factors Associated with the Mental Health of College Students." *Journal of American College Health,* 2012, 60(3), 185–193.

Curtis, C. "Youth Perceptions of Suicide and Help-Seeking: 'They'd Think I was Weak or "Mental."' *Journal of Youth Studies,* 2010, 13(6), 699–715.

Davidson, L., and Locke, J. H. "Using a Public Health Approach to Address Student Mental Health." In J. Kay and V. Schwartz (eds.), *Mental Health Care in the College Community.* West Sussex, UK: Wiley-Blackwell, 2010.

Eisenberg, D., Golderstein, E., and Gollust, S. E. "Help-Seeking and Access to Mental Health Care in a University Student Population." *Medical Care,* 2007, 45(7), 594–601.

Green, L. W. "Modifying and Developing Health Behavior." *Annual Review of Public Health,* 1984, 5, 215–236.

Green, L. W., and Kreuter, M. W. *Health Promotion Planning: An Educational and Environmental Approach*. (2nd ed.) Mountain View, Calif.: Mayfield, 1991.

Hayden, J. *Introduction to Behavior Change*. Sudbury, Mass.: Jones and Bartlett, 2009.

Jed Foundation and Education Development Center. *The Guide to Campus Mental Health Action Planning*, 2011. Retrieved September 15, 2012, from www.sprc.org/sites/sprc .org/files/library/CampusMHAP_Web%20final.pdf

Jed Foundation and Suicide Prevention Resource Center. *Model for Comprehensive Suicide Prevention and Mental Health Promotion*. n.d. Retrieved September 15, 2012, from www.jedfoundation.org/professionals/comprehensive-approach

Kessler, R. C., and others. "Life-time Prevalence and Age-of-onset Distribution of DSM-IV Disorders in the National Co-morbidity Survey Replication." *Archives of General Psychiatry*, 2005, 62, 593–602.

Keup, J. R. "New Challenges in Working With Traditional-Aged College Students." In B. O. Barefoot and M. Kramer (eds.), *The First Year and Beyond: Rethinking the Challenge of Collegiate Transition*. New Directions for Higher Education, no. 144. San Francisco: Jossey-Bass, 2008.

Kezar, A., and Eckel, P. D. "Meeting Today's Governance Challenges: A Synthesis of the Literature and Examination of a Future Agenda for Scholarship." *Journal of Higher Education*, 2004, 75(4), 371–399.

King, K. A., Vidourek, R. A., and Strader, J. L. "University Students' Perceived Self-Efficacy in Identifying Suicidal Warning Signs and Helping Suicidal Friends Find Campus Intervention Resources." *Suicide and Life-Threatening Behavior*, 2008, 38(5), 608–617.

Kitzrow, M. A. "The Mental Health Needs of Today's College Students: Challenges and Recommendations." *Journal of Student Affairs Research and Practice*, 2009, 46(4), 646–660.

Martin, J. M. "Stigma and Mental Health in Higher Education." *Higher Education Research and Development*, 2010, 29(3), 259–274.

McLeroy, K. R., Bibeau, D., Steckler, A., and Glanz, K. "An Ecological Perspective on Health Promotion Programs." *Health Education & Behavior*, 1988, 15(4), 351–377.

Megivern, D., Pellerito, S., and Mowbray, C. "Barriers to Higher Education for Individuals With Psychiatric Disabilities." *Psychiatric Rehabilitation Journal*, 2003, 26(3), 217–231.

Mowbray, C. T., and others. "Campus Mental Health Services: Recommendations for Change." *American Journal of Orthopsychiatry*, 2006, 76(2), 226–237.

National Cancer Institute. *Theory at a Glance: A Guide for Health Promotion Practice*. (2nd ed.), 2005. Retrieved June 27, 2011, from www.cancer.gov/cancertopics /cancerlibrary/theory.pdf

National Mental Health Association and the Jed Foundation. *Safeguarding Your Students Against Suicide: Expanding the Safety Net: Proceedings From an Expert Panel on Vulnerability, Depressive Symptoms, and Suicidal Behavior on College Campuses*, 2002. Retrieved August 16, 2011, from www.jedfoundation.org/assets/Programs/Program _downloads/SafeguardingYourStudents.pdf

Parrish, M., and Tunkle, J. "Clinical Challenges Following an Adolescent's Death by Suicide: Bereavement Issues Faced by Family, Friends, Schools and Clinicians." *Clinical Social Work Journal*, 2005, 33(1), 81–102.

Potter, L. B., Powell, K. E., and Kachur, S. P. "Suicide Prevention From a Public Health Perspective." *Suicide and Life Threatening Behavior*, 1995, 25(1), 82–88.

Quinn, N., Wilson, A., MacIntyre, G., and Tinklin, T. "'People Look at you Differently': Students' Experience of Mental Health Support Within Higher Education." *British Journal of Guidance & Counselling*, 2009, 37(4), 405–418.

Randazzo, M. R., and Plummer, E. *Implementing Behavioral Threat Assessment on Campus: A Virginia Tech Demonstration Project*. Blacksburg, Va.: Virginia Polytechnic Institute and State University, 2009.

Rihmer, Z., Belso, N., and Kiss, K. "Strategies for Suicide Prevention." *Current Opinion in Psychiatry*, 2002, *15*(1), 83–87.

Schneider, M. J. *Introduction to Public Health*. (3rd ed.) Sudbury, Mass.: Jones and Bartlett, 2011.

Siggins, L. D. "Working With the Campus Community." In J. Kay and V. Schwartz (eds.), *Mental Health Care in the College Community*. West Sussex, UK: Wiley-Blackwell, 2010.

Stokols, D. "Translating Social Ecological Theory Into Guidelines for Community Health Promotion." *American Journal of Health Promotion*, 1996, *10*(4), 282–298.

Suicide Prevention Resource Center. *Suicide Prevention: The Public Health Approach*, 2002. Retrieved August 16, 2011, from www.sprc.org/library/phasp.pdf

Suicide Prevention Resource Center. *Promoting Mental Health and Preventing Suicide in College and University Settings*, 2004. Retrieved August 16, 2011, from www.sprc.org /library/college_sp_whitepaper.pdf

Trela, K. "Facing Mental Health Crises on Campus." *About Campus*, 2008, *12*(6), 30–32.

U.S. Department of Health and Human Services Office of the Surgeon General and National Action Alliance for Suicide Prevention. *National Strategy for Suicide Prevention: Goals and Objectives for Action*, 2012. Retrieved September 15, 2012, from www .surgeongeneral.gov/library/reports/national-strategy-suicide-prevention/full_report -rev.pdf

U.S. Public Health Service. *The Surgeon General's Call to Action to Prevent Suicide*, 1999. Retrieved September 15, 2012, from http://137.187.25.243/library/calltoaction /calltoaction.pdf

Van Orden, K. A., and others. "Suicidal Ideation in College Students Varies Across Semesters: The Mediating Role of Belongingness." *Suicide and Life-Threatening Behavior*, 2008, *38*(4), 427–435.

Winslow, C.E.A. "The Untilled Fields of Public Health." *Science*, 1920, *51*(1306), 23–33.

World Health Organization. *Preamble to the Constitution of the World Health Organization as Adopted by the International Health Conference*, New York, June 19–July 22, 1946; signed on July 22, 1946, by the representatives of 61 States (Official Records of the World Health Organization, no. 2, p. 100) and entered into force on April 7, 1948. Retrieved August 8, 2011, from www.who.int/suggestions/faq/en/index.html

ELIZABETH C. JODOIN *is a staff counselor at the University of North Carolina at Greensboro (UNCG), as well as a doctoral student at UNCG pursuing her PhD in educational studies.*

JASON ROBERTSON *is an assistant professor at Averett University. Prior to this, he was the wellness coordinator for the Wellness Center at UNCG and served as the director of outreach and training on the school's SAMHSA Garret Lee Smith Grant.*

This chapter reviews factors in effective gatekeeper training as part of a comprehensive suicide prevention program. A case example is provided to illustrate the application of these factors.

Gatekeeper Training in Campus Suicide Prevention

Cory Wallack, Heather L. Servaty-Seib, Deborah J. Taub

College counseling center directors throughout the United States have reported significant increases in rates of both student use of mental health resources and the severity of presenting problems (Gallagher, 2008). However, while rates of use of resources are at record highs, most college students potentially at risk for suicide remain unknown to campus mental health professionals (Gallagher, Zhang, and Taylor, 2004). To increase the percentage of at-risk students engaged with campus mental health professionals, the Jed Foundation and the Suicide Prevention Resource Center (Silverman, Locke, and Davidson, 2007) recommend that campuses enhance the early identification of at-risk students as one of seven strategic components of a comprehensive suicide prevention program.

A range of strategies exists for identifying at-risk students, including requiring incoming students to complete medical history forms, conducting depression and anxiety screening days, and implementing broad-based online self-assessments. In addition to these strategies, gatekeeper training is one of the most commonly employed methods for identifying and intervening with at-risk students (Davidson and Locke, 2010). Within the context of campus suicide prevention, a gatekeeper is broadly defined as any individual who has the potential to come into contact with at-risk students (Davidson and Locke, 2010). Although the philosophy, content, and length vary, the underlying premise of all gatekeeper training programs is that

This chapter was developed, in part, under grant number 1H79SM057821-01 from SAMHSA. The views, opinions, and content of this publication are those of the authors and contributors, and do not necessarily reflect the views, opinions, or policies of CMHS, SAMHSA, or HHS, and should not be construed as such.

individuals within the community can be trained to recognize suicide warning signs, to question students about thoughts of suicide, and to refer at-risk students to mental health professionals (Tompkins, Witt, and Abraibesh, 2010).

In this chapter, we review systemic factors that are essential to consider when developing, implementing, and evaluating gatekeeper training. Consistent with recommendations for effective practices, we have structured the essential factors within a strategic thinking and planning model (Davidson and Locke, 2010). Our five-step strategic planning model consists of: assessing campus culture, assessing campus resources, selecting a training program, preparing the campus, and establishing and evaluating programmatic goals. To illustrate this strategic planning model, we conclude this chapter with a case example from Purdue University.

Research assessing the effectiveness of gatekeeper training has provided promising findings (for example, Cross, Matthieu, Lezine, and Knox, 2010; Isaac, Elias, and Katz, 2009). For example, among nonclinical department of psychiatry employees, gatekeeper training resulted in enhanced recognition of suicide warning signs, enhanced knowledge regarding how to intervene with someone thinking about suicide, and enhanced self-efficacy for responding to individuals in crisis (Cross, Matthieu, Cerel, and Knox, 2007). Additional studies have demonstrated the positive impact of gatekeeper training among secondary school staff (Wyman, Brown, and Inman, 2008), secondary school students (Stuart, Waalen, and Haelstromm, 2003), and veterans (Matthieu and others, 2008). Finally, recent studies have demonstrated effectiveness in enhancing knowledge (Cross, Matthieu, Lezine, and Knox, 2010) as well as skills and self-efficacy (Pasco, Wallack, Sartin, and Dayton, forthcoming) among campus gatekeepers.

Given the apparent need, and the growing body of research demonstrating its effectiveness, it may be tempting for campus administrators to eagerly implement gatekeeper training on their campuses. However, prior to implementation there are numerous variables administrators must consider to enhance the likelihood of gatekeeper training being successful. The implementation work required to support gatekeeper training may seem tedious and time consuming, and it may be appealing for administrators to overlook the implementation factors we will review in this chapter. However, much as decorating the interior of a newly constructed house is preceded by surveying the land, pouring the foundation, building support frames, and selecting the appropriate construction materials, effective suicide prevention programming requires the same attention to detail to ensure success and sustainability.

Step 1: Assessing Campus Culture

Consistent with discussion in previous chapters, it is our firm belief that gatekeeper training is only one element of a comprehensive public health approach to suicide prevention. Although a public health approach is the recommended strategy for comprehensive suicide prevention efforts, it is crucial for campus administrators to remember that a one-size-fits-all public health model does not exist and that intimate familiarity with one's own campus culture is necessary to develop programs that successfully address unique campus needs (Edwards and others, 2000). Given the importance of understanding the cultural context within which gatekeeper training will be implemented, the first step toward implementation is conducting an assessment of the campus culture. Specific variables to assess include: student body demographics, student behavioral and mental health, current help-seeking behaviors, and the campus values and attitudes toward mental health–related concerns.

Student Body Demographics. Understanding campus culture requires a thorough understanding of the campus population. Important information that can assist in developing a comprehensive understanding of the student population includes student demographic data such as age, race, gender, sexual orientation, socioeconomic status, and religion. Additional factors to consider include the number of veterans on campus, the percentage of residential students compared to commuter students, the number of international students, and the numbers of students who are involved with Greek life and athletic teams. Knowing the composition of the student population provides important guidance in determining the allocation of limited campus resources and will assist in identifying specific student populations who may be at greater risk and thus may benefit from more directed intervention efforts. Moreover, this information provides critical knowledge in terms of developing a culturally competent implementation plan. For example, on a campus with significant numbers of international students, it would be useful to consider developing program materials in multiple languages. Campus sources for information about student body demographics include Institutional Research, the registrar, and student life offices including Residence Life and Campus Activities. Annual surveys such as the Cooperative Institutional Research Program (CIRP) Freshman Survey, the College Senior Survey, Your First College Year (www.heri.ucla.edu/herisurveys.php), the Beginning College Survey of Student Engagement, and the National Survey of Student Engagement (nsse.iub.edu) also can supply a wealth of information about your students.

Student Behavioral and Mental Health. National data regarding rates of suicide ideation, suicide attempts, substance abuse, and other high-risk behaviors are available through resources such as the National College Health Assessment (American College Health Association, 2009) and the National Research Consortium of Counseling Centers in Higher Education (Drum, Brownson, Burton Denmark, and Smith, 2009). Such data provide important guidance for the effective implementation of gatekeeper training. For example, Drum, Brownson, Burton Denmark, and Smith (2009) reported that two-thirds of college students who disclosed suicidal ideation first told a peer and very rarely confided in a professor. Yet in our own experience working with campuses implementing gatekeeper training, program administrators often identify faculty as the primary target for gatekeeper training and overlook peers. This example demonstrates the need for program administrators to be familiar with available data and to use it accordingly in program development and implementation.

Although national data can provide important guidance, it is critical to obtain campus-specific data because campus data may differ from national data. Moreover, individuals participating in gatekeeper training generally prefer to be informed of campus-specific data rather than national data as it holds greater personal meaning. Participation in studies such as the National College Health Assessment or Healthy Minds (Eisenberg, Golberstein, and Gollust, 2007) allows for effective gathering of campus-specific data that can readily be compared to national data. Campuses that do not participate in such studies may consider conducting campus surveys to obtain this crucial information.

What Help-Seeking Behaviors Are Already Present? As the primary goal of gatekeeper training is identification and referral of at-risk students, it is crucial to have an understanding of help-seeking behaviors on campus prior to implementing gatekeeper training. Important questions to address include:

- What percentage of students currently access counseling services?
- What factors prevent help seeking?
- What factors promote help seeking?
- Are faculty, staff, and students aware of how to access counseling services?
- To what extent are faculty, staff, and students willing to intervene with at-risk students?

These questions can be assessed by conducting surveys or focus groups. When conducting such assessments, it is essential to obtain samples that accurately reflect the campus population, with particular emphasis placed on including representatives from populations known to use campus resources at lower rates than is appropriate.

Campus Values Toward Mental Health. Finally, administrators are advised to assess specific campus climate indicators that may affect the success of gatekeeper training programs. As with the assessment of help-seeking behaviors, this information can be obtained via surveys or focus groups. Questions to consider include:

- To what extent are individuals on campus fearful of students in crisis?
- To what extent does the campus culture maintain or affect stigma associated with mental health problems?

- Does the campus culture encourage help seeking or does it unintentionally discourage help seeking due to its inability to tolerate student distress?

Step 2: Assessing Resources

Having assessed campus culture, it is necessary to assess the campus resources available to support gatekeeper training. Three particularly important resources are: people, time, and counseling services.

People. In assessing the resource of people, two questions must be addressed:

- Who will conduct our gatekeeper training?
- Who will we train to be gatekeepers?

Although they represent a variety of professional backgrounds, gate-keeper trainers are most commonly mental health professionals, health educators, and graduate students in mental health fields. It is essential to have a sufficient number of trainers to meet the campus need as well as to ensure sustainability. Campuses with only one or two trainers frequently incur the problem of being unable to meet the demand for training. More-over, if these trainers leave the institution, gatekeeper training cannot continue until new trainers are identified. Therefore, it is essential that there be a sufficient number of trainers available from the onset of implementation.

Individuals who may be targeted as gatekeepers include residence life staff, chaplains, coaches, faculty, and students (Tompkins and Witt, 2009). In determining who gatekeepers will be, it is essential to rely on the information obtained when assessing the campus culture as these data indicate to whom students turn when they are in distress, and it is these individuals who may most benefit the campus by becoming trained gatekeepers.

Time. Among commercially available gatekeeper training programs, the required implementation time ranges from one hour to two days (Davidson and Locke, 2010). It is crucial to accurately assess the amount of time that targeted gatekeepers will be willing and able to commit. If a training model requires three hours to complete, but an intended audience is willing to commit only one hour, program administrators must consider a different (that is, shorter) training program or convince the target audience to commit a greater amount of time.

Counseling Services. The success of gatekeeper training depends not only on the intervention of gatekeepers but the availability of mental health resources to receive referrals from gatekeepers. Insufficient counseling services may place gatekeepers in the position of identifying at-risk students while leaving them lacking professional resources to which they can refer students. The International Association of Counseling Centers

(2010) recommends that counseling centers maintain a professional staff-to-student ratio of 1:1,500. Counseling centers that are above this ratio may find it difficult to manage the increased student usage that often coincides with gatekeeper training. Moreover, regardless of size, it is essential that counseling center staff be skilled in conducting risk assessments. Training programs such as the Suicide Prevention Resource Center's (SPRC) Assessing and Managing Suicide Risk or the American Association of Suicidology's Recognizing and Responding to Suicide Risk (Pisani, Cross, and Gould, 2011) have been demonstrated to be effective training models. Finally, in regards to counseling services, it is necessary to assess the availability of after-hours services. Although many counseling centers provide 24-hour coverage via crisis hotlines, on those campuses that do not have such a resource, it may be important to consider implementing such a resource or relying on existing resources such as the National Suicide Prevention Hotline or partnering with community crisis centers that offer telephone crisis counseling.

Step 3: Selecting a Gatekeeper Training Program

Having gained a sense of campus culture and campus resources, the next step in the strategic planning process is to select which gatekeeper training program to employ. There are numerous gatekeeper training programs commercially available. As a complete review of the various gatekeepers training models is beyond the scope of this chapter, readers are referred to the SPRC's Comparison Table of Suicide Prevention Gatekeeper Training Programs (Suicide Prevention Resource Center, 2011). For each gatekeeper training program, this resource summarizes the program's requirements, targeted audiences, program highlights, and program objectives. Campus administrators are encouraged to carefully consider their available resources and campus culture when determining which program to select. Campuses with financial limitations are encouraged to partner with other campuses as a means of combining resources and defraying potential costs.

Step 4: Preparing the Campus for Gatekeeper Training

Having selected which gatekeeper training program to use, the next strategic planning step is preparing the campus for implementation. Particular issues to address include obtaining institutional buy-in, ensuring that appropriate policies and procedures are in place, and generating community awareness that gatekeeper training will be implemented.

Institutional Buy-In. When seeking institutional buy-in, it is critical to remind senior administrators and a broad base of stakeholders that enhancing the mental health of the entire student population should be everyone's concern and responsibility (Davidson and Locke, 2010).

NEW DIRECTIONS FOR STUDENT SERVICES • DOI: 10.1002/ss

Presidents, chancellors, deans, department heads, and student leaders should be informed of pending gatekeeper training and asked to provide the needed support (for example, funding, public statements of support, provision of space) for success and long-term sustainability. When possible, it is particularly advantageous to invite senior-level administrators to become trained gatekeepers as their participation can promote campus involvement. Moreover, once training has been initiated, senior administrators should be provided regular updates regarding implementation progress as well as any relevant assessment reports.

While administrative involvement is helpful, a simultaneous bottom-up approach is recommended. For example, while having a dean's support may assist with faculty buy-in, it would be equally valuable to identify faculty who are motivated to become gatekeepers, as these individuals can generate support among colleagues and, in turn, encourage the support of senior administrators.

Ensuring That Appropriate Policies and Procedures Are in Place. During gatekeeper training sessions, trainees frequently ask, "What happens if an at-risk student refuses a counseling center referral?" To ensure programmatic success, campus administrators must answer this crucial question prior to implementing gatekeeper training. In recent years, there has been a significant increase in the use of mandated policies whereby potentially at-risk students are required to be assessed at the campus counseling center (Joffe, 2008). Although a review of such policies is beyond the scope of this chapter, it is important to consider the manner in which these mandated evaluation policies support gatekeepers. Likewise, behavioral intervention teams have increasingly been employed to address this concern (Flynn and Heitzmann, 2008). Although they vary by name, the purpose of such teams is to receive referrals from campus community members who are concerned about a student's well-being. It then becomes the behavioral intervention team's responsibility to determine appropriate action steps.

Generating Community Awareness That Gatekeeper Training Will Be Implemented. Numerous strategies exist for informing the community of plans to implement gatekeeper training. Program administrators are advised to write press releases, encourage the campus newspaper to write an article, provide campus-wide advertising, or hold a kickoff event to generate awareness and support. An additional strategy that can be particularly useful in generating community awareness is linking various public health approaches together through a larger marketing approach. Examples of such approaches include George Mason's comprehensive Mason Cares program, Syracuse University's Campus Connect, and Purdue University's ALIVE @ Purdue (reviewed in detail later in this chapter). The advantage of such an approach is that each individual element of the broader public health model will be naturally connected to other elements, thus maximizing community awareness.

Step 5: Establishing and Evaluating Programmatic Goals

In developing programmatic goals it is essential that program administrators establish objective, measureable goals that are consistent with the available resources, campus culture, and selected gatekeeper training program. Although the ultimate goal of any suicide prevention effort is the reduction of suicide deaths, the actual number of suicide deaths on any given campus is sufficiently low to make it nearly impossible to demonstrate significant changes in this variable, and even if such changes were demonstrated, it would be difficult to attribute the outcome of such a finding to a single intervention such as gatekeeper training. As such, alternative strategies for evaluating the effectiveness of gatekeeper training include participant satisfaction measures; changes in counseling center usage; increased campus referrals to counseling services; changes in gatekeepers' attitudes, knowledge, and skills; and changes in gatekeeper behavior. It is critical to remember that to measure change in these variables effectively, baseline data are needed, and, as such, assessment of these variables must occur prior to implementing gatekeeper training.

Case Study: ALIVE @ Purdue

To illustrate the systemic factors and steps reviewed throughout this chapter, we conclude with a case study of Purdue University's comprehensive suicide prevention project, ALIVE (Awareness Linking Individuals to Valuable Education) @ Purdue. Although ALIVE @ Purdue is a broad-based public health approach to suicide prevention, consistent with the theme of this chapter, we primarily have focused on the project's gatekeeper training component.

The overarching purpose of ALIVE @ Purdue was to reduce suicide and suicide attempts among at-risk Purdue University students by fostering campus-wide knowledge, skills, and attitudes that would promote help-seeking behaviors. The primary strategy employed to achieve this goal was enhanced early identification and referral of potentially at-risk students. A major facet of our strategy was gatekeeper training for resident assistants (RAs). The team determined the need to employ a theory with a strong empirical base with college students and decided on the Theory of Planned Behavior (TPB; Ajzen, 1991; now Theory of Reasoned Action, Fishbein and Ajzen, 2010). TPB asserts that intentions to engage in a behavior (for example, an RA's referring an at-risk student) are determined by attitudes toward the behavior, subjective norms (that is, how others would view the behavior), and perceived behavioral control or self-efficacy regarding the behavior. The theory is well suited for translating research into the development and implementation of training programs. This case study illustrates how the strategic planning process outlined above was implemented.

Step 1: Assessing Campus Culture

Student Body Demographics. Purdue is a large, research-intensive, and decentralized university with well-known science, technology, engineering, and mathematics programs. Unlike most institutions of higher education in the United States, the majority of Purdue undergraduates are male (59 percent); in fact, in contrast to national trends, the percentage of women students at Purdue has declined slightly over the past decade. Approximately 6 percent of Purdue undergraduates are international students; Purdue has the second-largest international student population of any public university in the United States. In terms of race or ethnicity, about 3.4 percent of the undergraduates at Purdue are African American, about 5 percent are Asian American, about 2.4 percent are Hispanic/Latino Americans, about 0.4 percent are Native American Indian, and about 88.7 percent are White.

Purdue University has the fourth-largest residence life system in the United States, with a housing capacity of 10,464 students and 1,014 apartments in family housing (and operating near or over capacity each year). Annually, about 90 percent of the entering first-year class lives in university residences. Of students living in residence halls, 61.2 percent are male and 38.8 percent are female; 67.1 percent are ages seventeen to nineteen, 25.8 percent are twenty to twenty-one, and 7.1 percent are twenty-two or older. By race, 68.4 percent are White, 7.8 percent are Asian American, 4.7 percent are African American, 2.8 percent are Hispanic/Latino, and 0.5 percent are Native American Indian. Of students living in residence halls, 10.1 percent are international students, primarily from Asia. The university residences population, therefore, in comparison to the campus population at large, provides an overrepresentation of men, minorities, and international students. The university residences population also overrepresents a younger population than the campus population at large. Both Institutional Research and University Residences were helpful sources of student demographic data.

Student Behavioral and Mental Health. Some insights into the needs of the general student population were provided by the annual CIRP Freshman Survey data. According to 2005 CIRP data, 23.6 percent of incoming first-time full-time first-year Purdue student respondents (13.8 percent of males and 36.5 percent of females) "frequently" felt "overwhelmed by all I have to do" in the past year and 5.7 percent reported "frequently" feeling depressed in the past year. Insights also were gained from the presenting concerns of clients at the campus counseling center. The two most prevalent presenting concerns of student clients at Counseling and Psychological Services (CAPS) were depression and anxiety.

What Help-Seeking Behaviors Are Already Present? The 2005 CIRP data revealed that only 4.9 percent of our entering first-year students estimated that the chances were very good that they would seek personal counseling while in college. In addition, it appeared (see figures in Counseling Services later in the chapter) that use of mental health resources was below what might be expected for a campus of 38,000 students.

We also explored attitudes on campus about referring distressed students to counseling. The team conducted a pilot study with Purdue RAs to determine which TPB-related beliefs (that is, attitudes, subjective norms, perceived behavioral control) were most predictive of RAs' intentions to refer at-risk students. Findings suggested that one belief highly associated with RAs' intention to refer an at-risk student was related to subjective norms, in that their fellow RAs, supervisors, and even their family and friends would approve of and want them to make such a referral. In addition, RAs' sense of their own ability to make a referral was also positively associated with their intention to refer an at-risk student (Servaty-Seib and others, forthcoming).

Campus Values Toward Mental Health. Purdue maintains a comprehensive, campus-based mental health service network including primary counseling services, outreach provision, and cooperative relationships between Purdue Police, Purdue Fire and Rescue, and community mental health providers and hospitals. In addition, the team concluded that the campus had a positive view of prevention and had invested resources into providing crisis-related services to students and information to family and friends regarding mental and behavioral health issues. The team members met with administrators in University Residences and Student Services prior to the grant submission and sought collaboration and support for the project.

Step 2: Assessing Resources

People. We decided to focus on training RAs as our gatekeepers. We chose to focus on students living in the residence halls because of the potential to make an impact on a large number of students (approximately 11,000 per year) and because certain at-risk populations (men, international students, students of color) were overrepresented in the resident population. To ensure that each of the approximately 300 RAs received gatekeeper training, we realized that we needed to be able to train all 300 of them during the same block of time during RA training. This meant that we needed a large number of trainers, so that training could be delivered to smaller groups, allowing for interactive activities. In connection with the review of campus resources and the team's desire to build capacity, graduate students in counseling were selected to serve as ALIVE @ Purdue educators. Through a train-the-trainer approach, graduate students received high-quality, crisis-related training while also learning how to effectively train gatekeepers. They received training about outreach and prevention, the mental and behavioral health needs of college students (with an emphasis on suicide risk and protective factors), and help-seeking behavior.

Time. Limitations addressed with regard to time arose in two particular areas as the team engaged in review and planning. First, although we initially anticipated training the educators during a regularly occurring graduate course, this option ultimately was not possible due to limited faculty resources and accreditation-related curricular demands. The team adapted by organizing an intensive train-the-trainers summer workshop. Second, we had hoped for three or four hours for training RAs. Through consideration of multiple factors and negotiation with University Residences, the team was allowed two hours to train new RAs and one and a half hours to train returning RAs. Based on the campus culture and the extent to which residential life at Purdue understandably protects their RA training time, the project team viewed this time allowance as an indication of trust and perceived value of the program.

Counseling Services. Purdue University has a solid mental health service network that includes the primary counseling services at CAPS and the Office of the Dean of Students (ODOS). Educational training facilities (such as the Purdue Counseling and Guidance Center), staffed by graduate student counselors-in-training, provide adjunct services to students and the community. Prior to the grant period, CAPS provided approximately 325 direct client service hours per week; the ODOS provided another approximately 112 hours of direct service per week; and the Purdue Counseling Guidance Clinic provided about 50 direct service hours per week. In addition, CAPS offers after-hours emergency service, and during the 2006–2007 academic year they received emergency contacts from 214 students.

We discussed the possibility that the implementation of the gatekeeper program could result in a greater number of students seeking counseling services; the counseling center made plans to increase the number of counseling groups in anticipation of this increase. They later also implemented a new triage system that enabled them to better respond to at-risk students.

Step 3: Selecting a Gatekeeper Training Program. The ALIVE @ Purdue team considered multiple factors in determining a gatekeeper framework and training material. The team struggled with the idea of developing our own materials. We realized as the planning year progressed that selecting an existing gatekeeper training program would be more efficient than developing our own program. Prior to reviewing the existing gatekeeper training programs, the team created an outline of the key elements it desired to have included in gatekeeper training. These elements included knowledge, attitudes toward help seeking and referral, experiential activities, and, perhaps most important, the infusion of data we had gathered about referral attitudes and behaviors. Members of the team reviewed available gatekeeper training programs.

The team determined that gatekeeper training provided to RAs needed to be consistent with the existing culture within University Residences and also aligned with the Purdue first-year students' limited openness toward seeking counseling services. The University Residences culture was highly focused on RAs "knowing their residents." The focus on interpersonal connection within Campus Connect was an excellent fit with the needs perceived by the ALIVE @ Purdue team.

The TPB elicitation study provided campus-specific information regarding the potential barriers that RAs perceived in referring at-risk residents to speak with a mental health professional. It was clear through the review of other gatekeeper training materials (for example, Question, Persuade, Refer), Campus Connect allowed for the greatest level of integration of these findings into the ALIVE @ Purdue RA training materials. Concerns about costs and concerns about the potential for sustainability of the gatekeeper training program after the grant was over also entered into our selection.

Step 4: Preparing the Campus for Gatekeeper Training

Institutional Buy-In. In anticipation of potential campus barriers associated with implementing RA gatekeeper training (for example, decentralized nature of institution), the ALIVE @ Purdue team developed an advisory board to provide perspective and guidance to the team. In creating this advisory board, particular care was given to including stakeholders from diverse backgrounds and offices, and stakeholders from major units (for example, University Residences, International Students and Scholars Office, Dean of Students) were invited to serve as members.

Ensuring That Appropriate Policies and Procedures Are in Place. The biggest questions raised by the trainers and the gatekeepers had to do with crises occurring after hours and on the weekend. We worked to understand the counseling center's policies and procedures about after-hours and weekend crises and University Residences' expectations about how RAs were to operate in these circumstances.

Generating Community Awareness That Gatekeeper Training Will Be Implemented. Our focus in terms of preparing the community was to network and communicate with multiple units and key staff members. More specifically, we were able to meet with our advisory board prior to even beginning training of the ALIVE @ Purdue educators and well before gatekeeper training was actually offered to RAs. Our careful selection of board members provided a natural flow of information back to campus offices highly invested in developing and enhancing campus suicide prevention efforts. In addition, during the grant application process, we acquired letters of support from administrators, who then prepared their staff members for the implementation of the gatekeeper training.

Step 5: Establishing and Evaluating Programmatic Goals. Issues of assessment were considered with the writing of the ALIVE @ Purdue grant and were further modified and adapted during the planning year. The team decided it was necessary to assess the effectiveness of the educators-in-training in their delivery of the Purdue Campus Connect program as well as changes in the RAs' communication skills and intentions to refer at-risk students.

The evaluation of educators-in-training suicide and crisis knowledge, attitudes, and skills necessary to be effective trainers was conducted using pre-post quantitative assessments and live observation (in addition to recording and review) of role-playing opportunities by the team. Empirically informed rubrics were developed to evaluate training and outreach skills (Taub and others, 2011). Results indicated significant improvement in educators' outreach presentation skills across all three training years (Taub and others, 2011). In addition, educators also displayed an increase in crisis communication skills (Wachter Morris and others, 2012).

The evaluation of the Purdue Campus Connect program provided to RAs was done through pre-post quantitative assessments of suicide and crisis knowledge and beliefs (that is, attitudes, subjective norms, perceived behavioral control) and behavioral intentions associated with referring at-risk students to speak with a mental health professional. In addition, RAs completed a general satisfaction with training form that included both items rated on a five-point scale and open-ended questions. Pre-post findings indicated that RAs involved in ALIVE @ Purdue improved in their crisis communication skills after receiving the Purdue version of Campus Connect as provided by graduate students serving at ALIVE @ Purdue Educators (Taub and others, forthcoming).

The team also collected more distal data potentially related to the gatekeeper training offered to RAs. More specifically, we developed a mental health referral form to be completed by RAs each time they referred an at-risk resident. We found that the staff of some residence halls was open to completing the form, but others were less consistent. Because the team had difficulty interpreting this inconsistent data, we ended the collection of the information halfway through the project. In addition, the team collected information prior to implementation (baseline) and at the end of each semester of the ALIVE @ Purdue regarding the number of campus suicide completions, number of suicide attempts, number of student seeking mental health services, the numbers of students accessing emergency services, and campus academic attrition.

Conclusion

Gatekeeper training can be an effective component of a comprehensive campus suicide prevention program. However, it is important that careful planning be done in advance of implementation to maximize the likelihood that implementation of such a program will be effective. As part of this planning, it is important to match the gatekeeper training program selected to the needs and culture of your particular campus.

References

Ajzen, I. "The Theory of Planned Behavior." *Organizational Behavior and Human Decision Processes*, 1991, *50*, 179–211.

American College Health Association. "College Health Assessment Spring 2008." *Journal of American College Health*, 2009, *57*, 485.

Cross, W. Matthieu, M. M., Cerel, J., and Knox, J. L. "Proximate Outcomes of Gatekeeper Training for Suicide Prevention in the Workplace." *Suicide and Life Threatening Behaviors*, 2007, *37*, 659–670.

Cross, W., Matthieu, M., Lezine, D., and Knox, K. "Does a Brief Suicide Prevention Gatekeeper Training Program Enhance Observed Skills?" *Crisis: The Journal of Crisis Intervention and Suicide Prevention*, 2010, *31*(3), 149–159.

Davidson, L., and Locke, J. H. "Using a Public Health Approach to Address Student Mental Health." In J. Kay and V. Schwarts (eds.), *Mental Health Care in the College Community*. London: Wiley, 2010.

Drum, D. J., Brownson, C., Burton Denmark, A., and Smith, S. E. "New Data on the Nature of Suicidal Crises in College Students: Shifting the Paradigm." *Professional Psychology*, 2009, *40*, 213–222.

Edwards, R. W., and others. "Community Readiness: Research to Practice." *Journal of Community Psychology*, 2000, *28*, 291–307.

Eisenberg, D., Golberstein, E., and Gollust, S. E. "Help Seeking and Access to Mental Health Care in a University Student Population." *Medical Care*, 2007, *45*, 594–601.

Fishbein, M., and Ajzen, I. *Predicting and Changing Behavior: The Reasoned Action Approach*. New York: Psychology Press, 2010.

Flynn, C., and Heitzmann, D. "Tragedy at Virginia Tech: Trauma and Its Aftermath." *Counseling Psychologist*, 2008, *36*, 479–489.

Gallagher, R. P. *National Survey of Counseling Center Directors*. The International Association of Counseling Services, University of Pittsburg, Series 8Q, 2008.

Gallagher, R. P., Zhang, B., and Taylor, R. "National Survey of Counseling Center Directors." (Monograph Series No.8N.) Alexandria, Va.: International Association of Counseling Services, 2004.

International Association of Counseling Services. *Standards for University and College Counseling Services*, 2010.

Isaac M., Elias B., and Katz L. "Gatekeeper Training as a Preventative Intervention for Suicide: A Systematic Review." *Canadian Journal of Psychiatry*, 2009, *54*(4), 260–268.

Joffe, P. "An Empirically Supported Program to Prevent Suicide in a College Student Population." *Suicide and Life Threatening Behaviors*, 2008, *38*, 87–103.

Matthieu, M., and others. "Evaluation of Gatekeeper Training for Suicide Prevention in Veterans." *Archives of Suicide Research*, 2008, *12*(2), 148–154.

Pasco, S., Wallack, C., Sartin, R. M., and Dayton, R. "The Impact of Experiential Exercises on Communication and Relational Skills in a Suicide Prevention Gatekeeper Training Program for Resident Advisors." *Journal of American College Health*, forthcoming.

Pisani, A., R., Cross, W. F., and Gould, M. S. "The Assessment and Management of Suicide Risk: State of Workshop Education." *Suicide and Life-Threatening Behaviors*, 2011, *41*, 255–276.

Servaty-Seib, H. L., and others. "Using the Theory of Planned Behavior to Predict Resident Assistants' Intention to Refer At-Risk Students to Counseling." *Journal of College and University Student Housing*, forthcoming.

Silverman, M. M., Locke, J. and Davidson, L. "Comprehensive Approach to Suicide Prevention and Mental Health Promotion." Presentation delivered at National Association of Student Personnel Administrators Mental Health Conference, Houston, Tex., 2007.

NEW DIRECTIONS FOR STUDENT SERVICES • DOI: 10.1002/ss

Stuart, C., Waalen, J., and Haelstromm, E. "Many Helping Hearts: An Evaluation of Peer Gatekeeper Training in Suicide Risk Assessment." *Death Studies*, 2003, 27, 321–333.

Suicide Prevention Resource Center. "Comparison Table of Suicide Prevention Gatekeeper Training Programs." Retrieved January 2011 from www.sprc.org/library/SPRC_Gatekeeper_Matrix.pdf

Taub, D. J., and others. "Developing Skills in Providing Outreach Programs: Construction and Use of the POSE (Performance of Outreach Skills Evaluation) Rubric." *Counseling Outcome Evaluation and Research*, 2011, 2, 59–72.

Taub, D. J., and others. "The Impact of Gatekeeper Training on University Resident Assistants." *Journal of College Counseling*, forthcoming.

Tompkins, T., and Witt, J. "The Short-Term Effectiveness of a Suicide Prevention Gatekeeper Training Program in a College Setting With Residence Life Advisers." *Journal of Primary Prevention*, 2009, 30(2), 131–149.

Tompkins, T. L., Witt, J., and Abraibesh, N. "Does a Gatekeeper Suicide Prevention Program Work in a School Setting? Evaluating Training Outcome and Moderators of Effectiveness." *Suicide and Life-Threatening Behavior*, 2010, 40, 506–515.

Wachter Morris, C. A., and others. "Integrating Curricular and Community Needs: The ALIVE @ Purdue Campus Suicide Prevention Program." Unpublished manuscript, April 11, 2012.

Wyman, P. A., Brown, C. H., Inman, J. "Randomized Trial of a Gatekeeper Program for Suicide Prevention: 1-Year Impact on Secondary School Staff." *Journal of Consulting and Clinical Psychology*, 2008, 76, 104–115.

CORY WALLACK *is director of the Syracuse University Counseling Center.*

HEATHER SERVATY-SEIB *is associate professor of educational studies and training director of the Counseling Psychology program at Purdue University.*

DEBORAH J. TAUB *is professor of higher education and coordinator of the Student Personnel Administration in Higher Education program at the University of North Carolina at Greensboro.*

This chapter explores the need and effectiveness of using peer educators to help address mental health issues on college campuses. The implementation process of a mental health peer education program at a large research institution, the University of North Carolina at Greensboro, is discussed.

Peer Education in Campus Suicide Prevention

Julie A. Catanzarite, Myles D. Robinson

Student peer educators have been used by higher education intuitions to influence the education and retention of college students for many years (Peck, 2011; Tinto, 1993), and most institutions have some type of peer educator program (Boyle, Mattern, Lassiter, and Ritzler, 2011; Brack, Millard, and Shah, 2008; Hunter, 2004). Newton and Ender (2010) broadly define the role of peer educators as "students who have been selected, trained, and designated by a campus authority to offer educational services to their peers. These services are intentionally designed to assist peers towards attainment of educational goals" (p. 6). Any peer educator program must include purposeful training, as well as clearly defined outcomes and procedures for peer educators (Wawrzynski, LoConte, and Straker, 2011). This is especially true for suicide prevention peer educators, as the topic is sensitive and involves the safety of student lives. In this chapter, the history and theories of peer education and the development and implementation of a peer education mental health and suicide prevention program at the University of North Carolina at Greensboro (UNCG) are discussed.

Peer Education in Higher Education

Today's peer education programs demonstrate the progress in which schools have adapted to meet the social, emotional, and educational needs

This chapter was developed, in part, under grant number SMO58453-02 from SAMHSA. The views, opinions, and content of this publication are those of the authors and contributors, and do not necessarily reflect the views, opinions, or policies of CMHS, SAMHSA, or HHS, and should not be construed as such.

of students. Nonetheless, peer education in its present form was not introduced until the 1960s, where early topics of peer-to-peer discussion and activism largely focused on topics of health and wellness, including influenza immunization, women's rights and contraception, and drug use (Sloane and Zimmer, 1993). In 1975, the founding of the BACCHUS Network at the University of Florida expanded these efforts through the development of formal programs for alcohol awareness and abuse prevention on college campuses (BACCHUS Network, 2011). Other peer health education topics gradually took hold during the 1980s and 1990s: substance abuse, sexual health, HIV/AIDS. More recently, mental health has increased as a focus of peer educator efforts, including Active Minds, the student mental health advocacy group.

Today, peer educators are specialized leaders and can assume such roles as resident assistant, peer counselor, ambassador, orientation leader, peer health educator, mentors, peer tutor, and student conduct adviser. Essentially, all peer educators, no matter their specific role on campus, are paraprofessionals (Newton and Ender, 2010). These students have some training and knowledge in a particular area, but not to the extent of professionals (Newton and Ender, 2010). The use of paraprofessionals is a cost-effective way for institutions to share important information, greatly influencing student wellness, retention, and academic success. Because of peer educators' strong and well-developed interpersonal and communication skills, these students are deemed "natural helpers" (Newton and Ender, 2010). Similarly, the National Peer Educator Survey reported that two-thirds of peer educators surveyed felt motivated by altruism to become peer educators (Wawrzynski, LoConte, and Straker, 2011).

Generally, research (Lockspeiser, O'Sullivan, Teherani, and Muller, 2008; Mattanah and others, 2010) has shown that peer educators are effective because they are perceived by other students as being like them enough to understand their problems and points of view. As a result, it becomes far easier for students to discuss sensitive information, such as sexual activity, that would most likely be awkward to discuss with an authority figure, in a safe and nonjudging peer environment.

Theories of Peer Education

Many social theories and models support the use of peer education as a means to promote healthy behaviors and critical decision making (Academy for Educational Development, 1996; Bandura, 1977; Goldstein, 1992; Perkins and Berkowitz, 1986; Roger, 1983; White, Park, Israel, and Cordero, 2009). Extensive research has shown that peers have the most significant influence on college students' growth and development (Astin, 1993; Pascarella and Terenzini, 2005).

According to social learning theory (Bandura, 1977, 1986), when given accurate information, individuals are very successful at empowering, modeling, and encouraging positive thought processes and behaviors in their peers. Also, Bandura (1986) argued that people learn from one another within specific social contexts, which ultimately leads to changes in behavior. Social learning theory also states that individuals need the knowledge and confidence to feel that their presence is significant in adding positive change to social contexts (Turner and Shepherd, 1999). In a similar way, Hogg and Vaughan (2002) stated that individuals use various identities that originate from membership in specific social contexts.

Peer educators have both structured and unstructured opportunities to observe and model credible and knowledgeable peer behaviors and outcomes. In turn, other students will try to model those behaviors in personal contexts and situations. Turner and Shepherd (1999) suggest that, because of their integration in various social networks, peer educators can model positive behaviors in various contexts and thus are extremely valuable and effective.

Rationale for a Suicide Prevention Peer Education Program

Institutional data at UNCG (American College Health Association, 2005, 2007) determined that students consider peer health educators to be more valid sources of health information than friends, resident assistants, television, magazines, and the Internet. In fact, 79.5 percent of students surveyed stated that they received information from a peer health educator, suggesting that this program had the potential to reach a large portion of the student body.

In addition, as mental health issues become a growing concern on college campuses across the nation (Daddona, 2011), targeted and specific programs are needed to address the lack of mental health awareness among students. Throughout the United States, targeted peer education training varied in topical focus from tobacco use prevention to sexually transmitted infection prevention (Wawrzynski, LoConte, and Straker, 2011); however, peer education training geared toward mental health promotion and suicide prevention has been noticeably absent.

At UNCG, specific areas of institutional concern included increasing student intakes at the counseling center, significant lack of awareness about mental health issues in general, and lack of awareness of campus services related to mental health. According to an unpublished survey administered in 2006, 75 percent of graduating students did not know about the university counseling center, and 92 percent reported that they did not receive any information on suicide prevention (American College Health Association, 2007). In addition, in UNCG's Healthy Minds Study (2008), 66 percent of students reported that they believed friends would reject them if they chose to receive mental health services, yet 96 percent of students agreed that they would support a peer receiving mental health services. This alarming information suggested a perceived stigma in talking about and receiving assistance for mental health issues at the institution, yet there clearly were peers who were willing to affirm help-seeking behaviors.

With a successful peer health education program in full force at the campus, and with the growing evidence supporting peer education as a means to disseminate accurate information, expanding the existing peer education program to address mental health awareness and suicide prevention seemed appropriate. A Garrett Lee Smith Campus Suicide Prevention grant enabled UNCG to launch this expansion. This new program became known as Friends Helping Friends.

The Mission of Friends Helping Friends

Peer educators in Friends Helping Friends serve as role models for all students by fostering a supportive environment for students experiencing thoughts of suicide and by facilitating access to campus resources. Friends Helping Friends established specific objectives toward achieving such a supportive, accessible environment by (1) raising general awareness about mental health issues, mental disorders, and warning signs of suicide; (2) mitigating stigma about mental health concerns and using counseling services; (3) promoting healthy, effective strategies for coping with mental health problems; and (4) implementing outreach initiatives that connect students with mental health resources and counseling professionals on campus (University of North Carolina at Greensboro, 2012).

Because of this focus on outreach and removing stigma, Friends Helping Friends is very different from a gatekeeper training program. Not only do peer educators go through many more hours of training, but they also have clearly defined roles on the college campus and actively participate in outreach events and presentations. Gatekeepers, although important in suicide prevention, are intended to act as identification and referral agents and might not participate in large campus outreach events.

Implementation of Friends Helping Friends

Each fall semester, potential peer educators were recruited through targeted marketing and asked to submit an application; candidates showing potential as peer educators were asked to come in for an interview. Accepted students participated in a three-credit course during the spring semester. In this introductory course, basic peer education skills such as listening, communication, boundaries, presentation skills, and conflict resolution were a priority. Health content also was discussed, including alcohol and other drugs, sexual health, nutrition and body image, domestic violence and masculinity, and sexual orientation and gender identity. Once students successfully completed the course, demonstrated knowledge of competencies, and successfully completed outreach on campus, they were asked to choose a specialty health area, all of which had been discussed in the introductory course. This course was a one-credit-hour option that specifically trained students to do outreach in a particular health area. Outreach by these specialty students included hosting awareness events on campus and completing classroom presentations, which were most often the academic success and college transition courses. Greek Life was another group often requesting educational health presentations.

In 2009, with the help of the Garrett Lee Smith grant from the Substance Abuse and Mental Health Services Administration, UNCG created a new mental health awareness and suicide prevention peer education specialty section. The content would fit seamlessly into the current program and would allow trained student leaders to reduce stigma on campus and provide accurate information about suicide to peers. Additionally, after training, these peer educators would be excellent referral sources and would clearly understand how their role differed from a professional staff member or licensed counselor.

The first year of the three-year grant involved gathering a team to write the curriculum and develop a student handbook, the first of its kind, which would be used as both a teaching tool and student resource book (University of North Carolina at Greensboro, 2012). To begin this process, key players from the institution, including a professor of higher education, a licensed psychologist, a health educator and professor of public health, two doctoral students, three master's students, and one undergraduate, provided diverse perspectives on the issues of mental health and suicide at the institution. The result of this combination allowed for a framework involving a mix of counseling, student affairs, and public health theories. The commonalities found among the research and an environmental scan of the institution became the basis for the curriculum. Within the literature, there was a strong focus on suicide risk and protective factors and how these may exhibit themselves differently in various student populations including student athletes, lesbian, gay, bisexual, and transgender (LGBT) students, and veterans. Understanding the barriers to receiving care also was a common theme in the literature. These topics all were addressed in the training handbook; in addition, the handbook included detailed instructions on how to help someone in crisis.

In August 2009, peer educators who had completed the introductory course and demonstrated an interest in mental health promotion and suicide prevention became the first students enrolled in Friends Helping Friends. Students showing an interest in this program were often social work, public health, education, or psychology majors. In the course, co-taught by a licensed psychologist from UNCG's counseling center and a graduate student from the higher education student affairs program, peer educators learned how to talk with individual students one on one, as well as how to conduct educational outreach promoting awareness of mental health and suicide among college students. In addition to assisting with outreach programs such as World Suicide Prevention Day and Depression

Screening Day, they also would help co-present an awareness presentation in the academic success and college transition courses, as well as in other courses such as physical education, psychology, and public health courses. The Friends Helping Friends presentation gave students a basic understanding of why mental health issues and suicide are so prominent on college campuses, while also giving students very basic tools on how to reach out to a friend.

The suicide prevention training for peer educators sought to develop three major skills sets: how to build a helping relationship with others, how to help themselves, and, finally, content knowledge related to mental health and suicide. Because peer educators tend to describe themselves as "natural helpers," peer educators need to be taught about the hazards of taking on something too big, internalizing others' problems, enabling unhealthy behaviors, attempting to do too much, and incurring legal liability (BACCHUS Network, 2008; Daddona, 2011). Because peer educators often are on the front lines, their training should necessitate empathetic listening, communication skills, and referral techniques. Given that troubled students are more likely to first seek assistance from other students than help from the campus support services (Sharkin, Plageman, and Manigold, 2003), training must teach helping skills because peer educators often are the first to respond.

Listening skills are essential in initially identifying students under mental duress (Daddona, 2011), and include attending to contradictory verbal messages while observing nonverbal behaviors (Okun and Kantrowitz, 2008) that could uncover stressors associated with suicide. Although all types of people are susceptible to suicide and the warning signs are consistent, the stressors that trigger symptoms of suicide vary among college students who identify with distinct cultures. Culture refers to the complicated, fluid influences of societal and personal assignments that affect identity, thoughts, and behaviors of groups of people (Newton and Ender, 2010). Identified as an at-risk population for suicide and typically socialized to suppress emotional distress, male college students are less likely to demonstrate help-seeking behaviors. Therefore, peer educators should be attentive to nonverbal behaviors, such as substance abuse and withdrawal, which may be associated with male students in distress (Zhang and others, 2005). Also considered as an at-risk population for suicide, students of color may experience stress due to the perceived and actual practices of prejudice and racism (Elmers and Pike, 1997; Smedley, Myers, and Harell, 1993). Other student populations, such as veterans, LGBT students, student athletes, creative arts majors, international students, distance learners, nontraditionally aged undergraduates, and postbaccalaureate students similarly require special consideration in suicide prevention training. For these reasons, peer educators need to understand the risk factors associated with diverse student backgrounds, as well as to adeptly address various populations in a culturally sensitive way.

In the context of suicide prevention, Friends Helping Friends peer educators would participate in a role-play, wherein two peer educators would alternate between the role of helper and the role of a student seriously contemplating suicide. The training exercise, designed to guide peer educators to confront behaviors indicative of suicide, consists of the helper observing the warning signs of suicide, verbalizing those observed verbal and nonverbal messages, and then directly asking clarifying questions, such as "Are you thinking of killing yourself?" and "Do you have a plan to kill yourself?" Newton and Ender (2010) place importance on peer educators' confronting or challenging discrepancies as a means for facilitating a helpful and honest helping encounter. Although the myth persists that mentioning suicide will somehow give someone the idea to attempt suicide, the reality is that someone experiencing suicidal feelings may feel relieved that someone finally recognized his or her emotional distress. Another myth suggests that nothing can be done to help suicidal people because they want to die. However, most people thinking about suicide are ambivalent and have conflicting emotions between life and death (Clayton, n.d.). Therefore, this specific role-play has been designed to provide peer educators with effective skills for observing, identifying, and confronting the warning signs of suicide, as well as to debunk myths associated with suicide.

Because students are apt to view peer educators as credible, reliable resources, and peer educators are instrumental in assisting distressed students along in their decision-making process, suicide prevention training should ensure that peer educators understand when, where, and how to connect students to the appropriate local and campus resources. Referral techniques for peer educators include listening carefully, knowing their limits, and seeking consultation (Daddona, 2011; Newton and Ender, 2010). The coordinators for Friends Helping Friends warn peer educators not to promise secrecy when students verbalize suicidal thoughts and that they must report suicide ideation immediately to counselors.

Results

After two semesters of piloting the Friends Helping Friends program, various assessments suggested both successes and areas needing improvement. From student journals embedded in the *Friends Helping Friends Handbook*, it became evident that the handbook itself was an essential tool, providing both information and a sense of confidence for the peer educators. In assessments given to students after each Friends Helping Friends outreach presentation, the results suggested that students continued to believe some of the myths often associated with suicide, such as talking about suicide causes suicide ideation. Instructors who had requested a Friends Helping Friends outreach presentation also indicated that students needed more tools—awareness was not enough to make a difference on campus. Students could sign up for SAFE Talk, a national research-based suicide prevention gatekeeper training that was brought to campus with the help of the grant funding, but it was not sustainable nor directly relatable to issues at UNCG. Taking these factors into consideration, a new campaign called I CARE—an acronym for Identify, Connect, Ask, Refer, Encourage— was developed to address the needs of students at UNCG.

I CARE was developed as a two-part program that expanded on the original outreach practices of Friends Helping Friends. Part one is a fifty-minute peer-led awareness presentation intended for classroom outreach that includes a brief skill development section; part two is a two-and-a-half-hour interactive presentation that provides a deeper understanding of suicide on the college campus and has a more intense skill development section. Provided a few times a year by a professional staff member, this presentation is a gatekeeper training intended for faculty, staff, students, or community members.

Considerations

Before implementing a suicide prevention peer education program on a campus, several considerations are needed. With any large-scale implementation project, support from other areas of the institution is essential. Any time an institution openly talks about mental health and suicide, the message sent to the public could be construed as otherwise stating, "The University of _____ is a 'suicide' school." No institution wants that type of publicity; thus, it becomes critical that the mission of the program be clearly and consistently communicated. In addition to the support from higher administration, cooperation from department-level administration becomes essential to the sustainability of the program. For example, at UNCG, the instructors of the academic success and transition course were encouraged to bring in Friends Helping Friends to fulfill the health and wellness component of the program. Other departments, such as the Dean of Students, Disability Services, Office of Multicultural Affairs, and Housing and Residence Life, among others, supported the Friends Helping Friends program during outreach events. This in itself sent a powerful message to students: this is an important topic, and we are here to support it and support you.

When implementing a suicide prevention peer education program, the selection of peer educators to join such a group can present some challenges. First, in the viewpoint of many students, talking about suicide may not be as exciting as talking to peers about sex or alcohol. We also discovered that students who wanted to give back to their peers had often been affected by a mental health concern—a friend who died by suicide or a personal struggle with depression or anorexia. Although this passion to help was generally supported in the Friends Helping Friends program, there was always the question: Is this student leader emotionally and mentally ready to talk openly with his or her peers about these sensitive issues?

In a similar way, during the very first session with peer educators, clear boundaries need to be set to suggest the discussion will primarily be about helping others, not oneself. These two guidelines, although not necessarily measurable, seemed to have a profound effect on the relationship and communication between the peer educators and the instructors.

At UNCG, distance education students were one population never reached by Friends Helping Friends. As with any support service, designing a peer education program that can reach these students can be a challenging task because peer relationships are often weak or nonexistent for distance learners.

Conclusion

From our experience, a suicide prevention peer education program can significantly affect the campus culture by helping to destigmatize talking about suicide and other mental health concerns. Taking the time to plan an effective training program has proven essential to the success of Friends Helping Friends. In addition, campus partnerships have had a profound impact on the institutionalization of peer health education upon grant completion. Friends Helping Friends has provided a safe venue to discuss mental health and suicide in an effective and productive manner that seeks to empower others, leading to a change in the overall culture of stigma around taboo topics.

References

Academy for Educational Development. *What Intervention Studies Say About Effectiveness*. Atlanta, Ga.: Centers for Disease Control and Prevention, 1996.

American College Health Association. *American College Health Association—National College Health Assessment: Reference Group Executive Summary, Fall 2004*. Baltimore: American College Health Association, 2005.

American College Health Association. *American College Health Association—National College Health Assessment: Reference Group Executive Summary, Fall 2006*. Baltimore: American College Health Association, 2007.

Astin, A. W. *What Matters in College: Four Critical Years Revisited*. San Francisco: Jossey-Bass, 1993.

BACCHUS Network. "Certified Peer Educator Student Leader Empowerment Training." Facilitator manual, 2008.

BACCHUS Network. "The BACCHUS Network Organization History." *BACCHUS Network*, 2011. Retrieved November 5, 2011, from www.bacchusnetwork.org/history .html

Bandura, A. *Social Learning Theory*. Englewood Cliffs, N.J.: Prentice Hall, 1977.

Bandura, A. *Social Foundations of Thought and Action*. Englewood Cliffs, N.J.: Prentice Hall, 1986.

Boyle, J., Mattern, C. O., Lassiter, J. W., and Ritzler, J. "Peer 2 Peer: Efficacy of a Course-Based Peer Education Intervention to Increase Physical Activity Among College Students." *Journal of American College Health*, 2011, 59(6), 519–529.

Brack, A. B., Millard, M., and Shah, K. "Are Peer Educators Really Peers?" *Journal of American College Heath*, 2008, 56, 566–568.

Clayton, P. J. "Suicide Prevention: Saving Lives One Community at a Time." *AFSP: Standardized Presentations on Suicide Prevention*, n.d. Retrieved September 30, 2012, from www.afsp.org

Daddona, M. F. "Peer Educators Responding to Students With Mental Health Issues." In L. B. Williams (ed.), *Emerging Issues and Practices in Peer Education*. New Directions for Student Services, no. 133. San Francisco: Jossey-Bass, 2011.

Elmers, M. T., and Pike, G. R. "Minority and Nonminority Adjustment to College: Differences or Similarities?" *Research in Higher Education*, 1997, *38*(1), 77–85.

Goldstein, M. S. *The Health Movement: Promoting Fitness in America*. New York: Twayne, 1992.

Healthy Minds Study. *2007 School Report: The University of North Carolina at Greensboro*. Ann Arbor, Mich.: Center for Student Studies, 2008.

Hogg, M. A., and Vaughan, G. *An Introduction to Social Psychology*. Sydney: Pearson, 2002.

Hunter, D. "Peer to Peer: Effective College Learning." *Change*, 2004, *36*(3), 40.

Lockspeiser, T. M., O'Sullivan, P., Teherani, A., and Muller, J. "Understanding the Experience of Being Taught by Peers: The Value of Social and Cognitive Congruence." *Advances in Health Science Education*, 2008, *13*, 361–372.

Mattanah, J. F., and others. "A Social Support Intervention to Ease the College Transition: Exploring Main Effects and Moderators." *Journal of College Student Development*, 2010, *51*(1), 93–108.

Newton, F. B., and Ender, S. C. *Students Helping Students*. (2nd ed.) San Francisco: Jossey-Bass, 2010.

Okun, B. F., and Kantrowitz, R. E. *Effective Helping: Interviewing and Counseling Techniques*. (7th ed.) Belmont, Calif.: Brooks/Cole, 2008.

Pascarella, E. T., and Terenzini, P. T. *How College Affects Students: A Third Decade of Research*. San Francisco: Jossey-Bass, 2005.

Peck, A. "In Practice: Peer Involvement Advisors Improve First-Year Student Engagement and Retention." *About Campus*, 2011, *16*(3), 22–25.

Perkins, H. W., and Berkowtiz, A. D. "Perceiving the Community Norms of Alcohol Use Among Students: Some Research Implications for Campus Alcohol Education Programming." *International Journal of Addiction*, 1986, *21*, 961–976.

Roger, E. M. *Diffusion of Innovations*. (3rd ed.) New York: Free Press, 1983.

Sharkin, B. S., Plageman, P. M., and Manigold, S. L. "College Student Response to Peers in Distress: An Explanatory Study." *Journal of College Student Development*, 2003, *44*(5), 691–698.

Sloane, B., and Zimmer, C. G. "The Power of Peer Health Education." *Journal of American College Health*, 1993, *41*(6), 241–245.

Smedley, B. D., Myers, H. F., and Harell, S. P. "Minority-Status Stresses and the College Adjustment of Ethnic Minority Freshmen." *Journal of Higher Education*, 1993, *64*(4), 434–452.

Tinto, V. *Leaving College: Rethinking the Causes and Cures of Student Attrition*. Chicago: University of Chicago Press, 1993.

Turner, G., and Shepherd, J. "A Method in Search of a Theory: Peer Education and Health Promotion." *Health Education Research*, 1999, *14*(2), 235–247.

University of North Carolina at Greensboro. *Friends Helping Friends Handbook*. Denver, Colo.: BACCHUS Network, 2012.

Wawrzynski, M. R., LoConte, C. L., and Straker, E. J. "Learning Outcomes for Peer Educators: The National Survey on Peer Education." In J. B. Williams (ed.), *Emerging Issues and Practices in Peer Education*. New Directions for Student Services, no. 133. San Francisco: Jossey-Bass, 2011.

White, S., Park, Y. S., Israel, T., and Cordero, E. D. "Longitudinal Evaluation of Peer Health Education on a College Campus: Impact on Health Behaviors." *Journal of American College Health*, 2009, *57*(5), 497–506.

Zheng, J., and others. "Gender Difference in Risk Factors for Attempted Suicide Among Young Adults: Findings from the Third National Health and Nutrition Examination Survey." *Annals of Epidemiology*, 2005, 15(2), 167–174.

JULIE A. CATANZARITE *is the student retention manager for Student Services at Forsyth Technical Community College.*

MYLES D. ROBINSON *is a professional adviser in the School of Engineering and Applied Science of the George Washington University.*

This chapter explores the intersection of mental health concerns and suicide of LGBT college students on campus, including bullying and cyberbullying. One campus's approach to providing support for these students is discussed.

Suicide Prevention for LGBT Students

R. Bradley Johnson, Symphony Oxendine, Deborah J. Taub, Jason Robertson

Extensive media coverage of the suicide deaths of several gay and lesbian youth (including Rutgers University student Tyler Clementi) has highlighted lesbian, gay, bisexual, and transgender (LGBT) youth as a population at-risk for suicide. In addition, it has caused colleges and universities to address mental health and suicide behavior among this very diverse college population. One issue that researchers, administrators, and students alike must address is how to delineate the membership of this population. Depending on whom you ask, the letters involved can be as long as LGBTTTQQIPAAA. The literature reviewed for this chapter used a variety of terms from LGBTQ to sexual minority and used various definitions to determine membership within these groups. We use the term *LGBT* unless we are referring specifically to a subpopulation within this group.

In this chapter, we review the research about LGBT suicide, risk factors and protective factors for LGBT students, and bullying and cyberbullying. The chapter concludes with a description of how one institution addressed suicide prevention for LGBT students.

Over the past three decades, research on the experiences of LGBT youth has increased substantially within education, especially within secondary education. Despite this increase, gauging the number of LGBT students in higher education is difficult. However, one source, a survey by the American College Health Association (2010), indicates that 7.2 percent of

This chapter was developed, in part, under grant number SMO58453-02 from SAMHSA. The views, opinions, and content of this publication are those of the authors and contributors, and do not necessarily reflect the views, opinions, or policies of CMHS, SAMHSA, or HHS, and should not be construed as such.

U.S. college students identify themselves as lesbian, gay, or bisexual. Beemyn (2003) noted that "there is no accurate measure of the number of transgender college students (just as there are no reliable statistics on the number of lesbian, gay, and bisexual students)" (p. 34); however, it is likely that there are a few transgender students on every college campus (Carter, 2000).

There are no authoritative data on suicide rates among LGBT persons because this information is not typically reported in death certificates. Therefore, it is necessary to look at mental health concerns, suicide ideation, and suicide attempts among LGBT persons. The literature shows a prevalent relationship between mental health issues, suicidal ideation, and suicide and sexual orientation and sexual identity within the LGBT population. Lesbian, gay, and bisexual (LGB) young people typically report higher levels of depression (D'Augelli, 2002; Westefeld, Maples, Buford, and Taylor, 2001) and substance abuse (Bontempo and D'Augelli, 2002), both of which are associated with suicidality (Russell and Joyner, 2001) (see Chapter 1). Other researchers have found that LGB college students are more lonely, more depressed, and endorse fewer reasons for living than their heterosexual peers (Westefeld, Maples, Buford, and Taylor, 2001). Data indicate that LGB young people are more likely than their peers both to consider and to attempt suicide (D'Augelli, Hershberger, and Pilkington, 2001; Russell and Joyner, 2001). A 1989 study reported that LGB youth were "two to three times more likely to attempt suicide than other young people and might comprise up to 30% of completed youth suicides annually" (Eisenberg and Resnick, 2006, p. 662), and Russell and Joyner (2001) found that LGB adolescents were more than twice as likely to attempt suicide than their heterosexual peers. Other studies have found that about half of the LGB participants have thought about suicide (D'Augelli, Hershberger, and Pilkington, 2001) and that 33–45% of LGB respondents have attempted suicide (Child Welfare League of America, 2009; D'Augelli, Hershberger, and Pilkington, 2001; Eisenberg and Resnick, 2006).

Although LGBT students usually are categorized together as "sexual minority" students, the "T" is really quite different from the "LGB." Whereas the terms *lesbian, gay*, and *bisexual* refer to sexual orientation (to whom one is attracted), the term *transgender* refers to gender identity (the gender one considers oneself) (Diamond, 2002; Grossman and D'Augelli, 2007). Transgender youth have been less studied than their LGB peers. However, one study of transgender youth (Grossman and D'Augelli, 2007) found that almost half of the participants had considered suicide seriously and that one fourth had attempted suicide.

In one of the largest studies of mental health issues and sexual orientation, Oswalt and Wyatt (2011) noted that the LGBT population was more at risk for mental health issues, not because they are members of this sexual minority group, but as a result of "environmental responses to their sexual orientation" (p. 1257). Navigating being a member of the LGBT community can be difficult for many youth. According to Morrow (2004),

"GLBT adolescents must cope with developing a sexual minority identity in the midst of negative comments, jokes, and often the threat of violence because of their sexual orientation and/or transgender identity" (pp. 91–92) and that, given the pervasive homophobia in our culture and in the families of LGBT youth, "the internalization of homophobic and heterosexist messages begins very early—often before GLBT youth fully realize their sexual orientation and gender identity" (p. 92). In addition, it is just recently that youth have been able to see role models in prominent roles on television with whom they can identify.

Despite advances in coverage of gay rights concerns in the media and the recent addition of more LGBT characters in the media, there is still a stigma around being LGBT. This stigma allows society to continue to devalue and discredit being LGBT relative to being straight or heterosexual or cisgender. It is the embodiment of this stigma by institutions, such as colleges and universities, and non-LGBT individuals' internalization of this stigma that can lead to heterosexism and thus result in prejudice (Herek, Chopp, and Strohl, 2007). As a result of stigma and prejudice, members of the LGBT community report higher levels of social stressors that result in higher rates of mood, anxiety, and substance abuse disorders (Meyer, 2003). In addition, social stressors from stigma and prejudice can lead to some members of the LGBT community to reject their own identity, be bullied, or experience discrimination.

Researchers have referred to the idea of "gay-related stress" (Bontempo and D'Augelli, 2002; Heck, Flentje, and Cochran, 2011; Kitts, 2005; Rotheram-Borus, Hunter, and Rosario, 1994) or "minority stress" (Meyer, 1995, 2003), that is, stressors that are unique to LGBT individuals and are related to coming out; discovery of being lesbian, gay, bisexual, or transgender; or being victimized for being LGBT. Also related to this gay-related stress is " 'institutional discrimination' resulting from laws and public policies that create inequities or omit LGBT persons from benefits and protections afforded others" (U.S. Department of Health and Human Services Office of the Surgeon General and National Action Alliance for Suicide Prevention, 2012, p. 122). Studies have found that internalized homophobia and victimization and gay-related stress can lead to psychological distress and other mental health concerns that may in turn contribute to overall suicidal ideation and behavior (Igartua, Gill, and Montoro, 2003; Meyer, 1995; Suicide Prevention Resource Center, 2008). This risk may be heightened by the lack of coping skills and protective factors that promote resilience, such as family and peer support and access to both physical and mental health providers (Suicide Prevention Resource Center, 2008).

Risk and Protective Factors

Risk factors for suicide are "characteristics that make it more likely that a person will think about suicide" or attempt suicide (U.S. Department of

Health and Human Services Office of the Surgeon General and National Action Alliance for Suicide Prevention, 2012, p. 13). Protective factors, in contrast, are characteristics that promote resilience and make suicide less likely (U.S. Department of Health and Human Services Office of the Surgeon General and National Action Alliance for Suicide Prevention, 2012). Suicide prevention efforts attempt to reduce risk factors and increase protective factors.

One of the reasons that LGBT students are more at risk for suicide than their heterosexual peers is that LGBT students experience greater prevalence of suicide risk factors (Eisenberg and Resnick, 2006). LGBT students exhibit higher levels of substance abuse (Bontempo and D'Augelli, 2002; Rosario, Schrimshaw, Hunter, and Gwadz, 2002; Russell and Joyner, 2001) and depression (Russell and Joyner, 2001; Safren and Heimberg, 1999). LGBT students also experience higher rates of parental and peer rejection (Ryan, Huebner, Diaz, and Sanchez, 2009) and parental and peer physical and verbal abuse (Grossman and D'Augelli, 2007). Having a family member or friend who has attempted suicide or has died by suicide also is a risk factor for suicide. Research indicates that LGB young people are more likely to have a friend who has attempted suicide than are their heterosexual peers (D'Augelli, Hershberger, and Pilkington, 2001). Harassment and bullying in schools has been linked to suicide (Bontempo and D'Augelli, 2002; Rivers, 2004). Rankin (2003) found that more than one-third of LGBT undergraduates had experienced harassment during the previous year, and 20 percent of respondents feared for their physical safety.

Risk factors for suicide that have been identified for transgender individuals include reporting depression, having a history of substance abuse, being under twenty-five years old, being forced into sex, and feeling victimized and being discriminated against based on gender (Clements-Nolle, Marx, and Katz, 2006). Other risk factors for suicide among transgender persons are similar to those for LGB students: parental rejection, substance abuse, peer victimization, and family violence (Grossman and D'Augelli, 2007).

There is relatively little research on protective factors for LGBT students (Suicide Prevention Resource Center, 2008). Eisenberg and Resnick (2006) identified three protective factors in their study of middle school and high school LGB students: family connectedness, caring adults, and school safety. Other protective factors for LGBT students include support from parents and peers (D'Augelli, 2002; Heck, Flentje, and Cochran, 2011; Kidd and others, 2006), the presence of Gay Straight Alliance organizations in their educational settings (Heck, Flentje, and Cochran, 2011), positive sexual or gender identity (U.S. Department of Health and Human Services Office of the Surgeon General and National Action Alliance for Suicide Prevention, 2012), and access to culturally appropriate mental health services (U.S. Department of Health and Human Services Office of the Surgeon General and National Action Alliance for Suicide Prevention, 2012).

NEW DIRECTIONS FOR STUDENT SERVICES • DOI: 10.1002/ss

Bullying

Bullying and cyberbullying have received a great amount of attention in the media as a result of recent deaths by suicide of a number of teens and young adults within the past few years. Bullying is defined as a behavior that (1) is intended to harm or disturb another, (2) occurs repeatedly over time, and (3) is imbalanced in terms of power (Nansel and others, 2001). The power described in this definition can be real or perceived and is exercised by a more powerful person or group over another (Ericson, 2001). Bullying may be verbal, physical, or psychological. Table 5.1 describes some of the direct and indirect forms of each type of bullying behavior (Berman, 2010). For many, bullying starts early, with approximately 5 million children in elementary and junior high school being affected each year (Blumenfeld and Cooper, 2010). Additionally, between 10 and 15 percent of young persons report being a victim of bullying on a regular basis (Blumenfeld and Cooper, 2010).

Until recently, there has been little study of bullying on college campuses and few statistics on LGBT students on college campuses experiences. The lack of statistics on LGBT students is further increased given that institutions of higher education typically do not collect demographic information such as sexual orientation or gender identity or expression from their students. Based on data from the State of Higher Education Report (Rankin, Blumenfeld, Weber, and Frazer, 2010), LGBT students reported being the victim of many types of harassment. In total, 23 percent of LGBT students, faculty, and staff reported being the victim of some form of harassment (Rankin, Blumenfeld, Weber, and Frazer, 2010). Harassment included having derogatory remarks made about them (61.1 percent), feeling deliberately ignored or excluded (47.0 percent), feeling isolated or left out (40.0 percent), feeling intimidated or bullied (30.1 percent), fearing for

Table 5.1. Direct and Indirect Forms of Bullying

	Direct	Indirect
Verbal	• Insulting language • Name calling • Ridicule • Cruel teasing or taunting rumors	• Persuading another to verbally abuse someone • Spreading malicious rumors • Anonymous phone calls • Offensive text messages and e-mails • Demeaning content on Web sites
Physical	• Striking, kicking • Throwing objects • Slapping, shoving • Using weapons	• Deliberately and unfairly excluding someone • Removing and hiding things
Gestural	• Threatening gestures • Staring at someone	• Repeatedly turning away

Used with permission from Berman (2010).

their physical safety (12.7 percent), being the victim of a crime (3.3 percent), or being the target of physical violence (3.2 percent). In addition, one-third of LGBT students, faculty, and staff have considered leaving their institution due to perceiving a hostile climate (Rankin, Blumenfeld, Weber, and Frazer, 2010).

With the advent of technology and new technologies coming about daily, cyberbullying has become a real concern as of late. Cyberbullying is defined as the use of computers, cell phones, and other technology to intentionally and repeatedly harm another (Hinduja and Pathcin, 2008). Students who identified as a member of the LGBT community are more likely to have been or to know someone who has been a victim of cyberbullying or have had negative information posted about them online (MacDonald and Roberts-Pittman, 2010). MacDonald and Roberts-Pittman (2010) found that 38 percent of college students had known someone who was a victim of cyberbullying, 21.9 percent had been a victim themselves, and 8.6 percent had cyberbullied someone else. MacDonald and Roberts-Pittman (2010) also found that 25 percent of college students reported they had been harassed through a social networking site, 21.2 percent had received harassing text messages, and 9.9 percent had had embarrassing things posted about them in a chat room.

It is interesting to note, however, that LGBT students do not report higher levels of victimizations than their heterosexual peers, perhaps due to the constant negative online interactions LGBT students may receive and the desensitization that may occur. This may lead to a decreased perception of negative interactions as cyberbullying, thereby leaving LGBT students particularly vulnerable to these actions (MacDonald and Roberts-Pittman, 2010). This can be particularly problematic because many LGBT youth can become socially isolated and explore their sexuality virtually through the use of the Internet and other technologies in an effort to find accepting and supportive peer and support groups (Brown, Maycock, and Burns, 2005; Hillier, Kurdas, and Horsley, 2001; McFarlane, Bull, and Rietmeijer, 2002). Many tend to choose this avenue because of the perceived privacy and ease of finding a supportive environment (Hillier, Kurdas, and Horsley, 2001). Given this, sites like Facebook and MySpace have been embraced by youth and young adults, especially those in the LGBT community (Egan, 2000; Hillier, Kurdas, and Horsley, 2001; Koblin, 2006). These sites allow students to interact and explore their identities in a perceived safe environnment (Maczewski, 2002).

Figure 5.1 explains how bullying, mental health concerns, and suicide are connected. Persons with a preexisting vulnerability (that is, disability, Asperger syndrome, member of a minority group) are often singled out. This means they are viewed as vulnerable by others in a given population. This then "invites" or leads to behavior on the part of one group or individual to exercise power over (bullying) this vulnerable individual, thereby leading to victimization. Table 5.1 lists some of the ways this occurs.

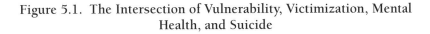

Figure 5.1. The Intersection of Vulnerability, Victimization, Mental Health, and Suicide

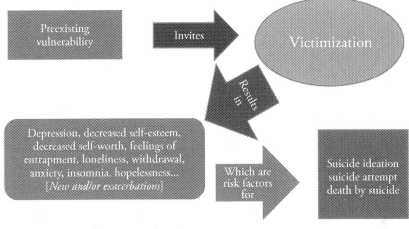

Used with permission from Berman (2010).

Victimization can lead to increased feelings of or manifestation of mental health concerns such as loss of self-worth, depression, and anxiety. As noted in Figure 5.1, all of these are risk factors for suicidal behavior. This is important to note, as being a member of the LGBT community or a victim of bullying does not automatically mean that one will become engaged in suicidal behavior.

Training

Most colleges and universities strive to create a safe and welcoming environment for all members of their community. Many colleges and universities have begun to see a growing enrollment among LGBT students. Resources such as Campuspride.com and Princeton Review's *Gay and Lesbian Guide to College Life* have made it easier for prospective students to identify welcoming campus environments.

Creating a welcoming campus involves increasing the ability and willingness of faculty, staff, and students to interact with students regardless of their identity. At the heart of this process is learning, which is defined as a change in cognition, usually permanent, that has an influence on behavior (Blanchard and Thacker, 2007). Learning comes in many forms and includes a person's knowledge, skills, and attitudes. One means of helping people gain new knowledge, skills, and attitudes is through training.

Diversity training is unique in its implementation. Awareness and knowledge are areas of great concern when addressing issues related to diversity but perhaps one of the greatest areas is that of self-efficacy.

NEW DIRECTIONS FOR STUDENT SERVICES • DOI: 10.1002/ss

Self-efficacy is defined as a belief of an individual to produce a given level of performance in a given domain (Bandura, 1994). Diversity self-efficacy thus addresses an individual's overall level of confidence in his or her ability to gain and use knowledge, skills, and attitudes to respond to diversity concerns and issues appropriately and aid in promoting a positive climate for diversity (Combs, 2002). Diversity trainings must, therefore, include mastery, modeling, and observational learning experiences that allow for persons to practice skills and identify and address mistakes as part of the transfer of skills back to a person's life (Combs, 2002). Diversity trainings thus allow for the empowerment of participants to produce change in their organization and affect their own personal judgment (Combs, 2002). This type of self-efficacy is paramount to persons working with LGBT students, faculty, and staff and must be incorporated in trainings.

Institutional Example

The University of North Carolina at Greensboro (UNCG) has a history of working toward equity and inclusion for its LGBT students, faculty, and staff. The Safe Zone program at UNCG was established in 2000 to educate and train allies (students, faculty, and staff) to provide a safe, comfortable, and supportive environment for LGBT and questioning individuals within the campus community, approximately 12 percent of whom identify themselves as LGBTQ, according to the 2011 American College Health Assessment results at UNCG. Safe Zone trainings were held every fall semester; a second training was added during the spring semester beginning in 2009 to meet the high demand for participation. This same year, program coordinators also established a train-the-trainer program and trained several campus members (currently thirty-two trainers) to serve as facilitators for Safe Zone programs to meet the high demand for the training sessions. Safe Zone participants attend a daylong workshop addressing a variety of topics and issues related to the LGBTQ community. At the end of the training, participants receive a certificate of completion, a Safe Zone sticker to display at their office, and a Safe Zone pin to wear to show their commitment to providing a comfortable environment for LGBTQ members of the community.

Since its establishment, Safe Zone has trained over 900 allies for the LGBTQ community. Almost 5,000 students, faculty, staff, and community members have attended Safe Zone programming events over the course of twelve years.

UNCG recently earned four and a half out of five stars on the LGBT-Friendly Campus Climate Survey sponsored by Campus Pride, which ranks areas of policy inclusion, support and institutional commitment, academic and student life, housing, campus safety, counseling and health, and recruitment and retention efforts of the institution.

NEW DIRECTIONS FOR STUDENT SERVICES • DOI: 10.1002/ss

UNCG, emphasized training in addressing suicide prevention for LGBT students. Training took various forms and involved multiple stakeholders and was based on the principles mentioned above. Training was not simply a onetime educational endeavor, but was an ongoing process that involved improving the overall knowledge, skills, and attitudes of participants. The multiple stakeholders involved in these trainings included students, faculty, staff, and community members in an effort to develop a network of support for those who identified as members of the LGBT community at UNCG.

Training opportunities were offered in train-the-trainer, workshop, and semester-long training styles. Although all training styles had a focus on the LGBT community, each had its own objectives. Each of these trainings was funded by grants from either the Guilford Green Foundation, the Adam Foundation, or the Garrett Lee Smith grant from the Substance Abuse and Mental Health Services Administration. (The Adam Foundation and the Guilford Green Foundation are two local LGBT service organizations that provide grants to LGBT-serving groups.) The train-the-trainer series focused on developing advocates and helping build the efficacy of people to be able to deliver presentations to the campus and surrounding community on issues facing the LGBT community, including mental health and bullying. The workshops were aimed at developing allies for the LGBT community who could serve as liaisons to the university as well as help take a stand on matters of injustice. The semester-long trainings focused on training students to help other students, thereby creating student peer educators who were able to meet their peers where they were and assist them as needed in getting assistance and reducing stigma around LGBT and mental health concerns. It is important to note that the trainers for these initial training styles were professionals in the field of LGBT health, student affairs professionals, or professionals in the field of health education. However, a trainer can be defined as anyone responsible for the delivery of instructional material (Lawson, 2010).

The first training focused specifically on LGBT mental health and suicide. For this training, we contracted with the Youth Suicide Prevention Program (YSPP) out of Washington State. This organization started in 1995 as a program under the Washington State Department of Health and became an independent 501(c)(3) in 2000 (Youth Suicide Prevention Program, n.d.). Since then, they have become locally and nationally recognized in the area of youth suicide prevention. The grant allowed UNCG to bring in their LGBT program coordinator for a presentation on suicide, bullying, and LGBT students. YSPP provided a two-tiered training. One training focused on raising awareness about LGBT youth and suicide risk. The other training was a train-the-trainer program. The train-the-trainer program covered factors that affect mental health concerns of LGBT youth, risk and protective factors, statistics related to LGBT youth suicide, and how to address suicide concerns. This training used several real stories from students who had experienced hardships as a result of their sexual orientation or gender identity and case studies on how particular cases were handled. Each of these allowed participants to engage in dialogue and practice addressing particular concerns that may arise on the college campus. Participants were given the PowerPoints, handouts, and training tips handouts. In addition, how a presentation was to be presented was role-played, along with the potential pitfalls and concerns that may arise in the training. Some of the anticipated concerns that were discussed were how to address difficult questions related to religion, choice versus "born this way," and so on.

The purpose of offering the YSPP trainings was to increase the overall self-efficacy of participants to address LGBT-related concerns on the campus. The train-the-trainer series was designed to help create advocates on the campus who could then help create an open and affirming campus culture. Given this information, each of the train-the-trainer programs looked to meet participants where they were and helped to develop their diversity self-efficacy. These types of trainings are a type of metatraining that allows you to model what it is you are asking participants to do (Biech, 2009).

The next train-the-trainer program grew out of the Safe Zone program offered through the university. The Safe Zone program, which had been in existence for eleven years, was getting inundated with requests to not only have its annual trainings, but also provide mini-trainings and outreach activities for the campus. As a result, one of the coordinators, along with the assistance of a graduate assistant, developed the idea of a train-the-trainer model. This program was aimed at members of the university community, students, faculty, and staff, who were already trained through the Safe Zone program. In addition, there was an overall application process through which a person's diversity self-efficacy was assessed prior to admission to the program. Although the aim is to increase self-efficacy, it was important to have persons who had a moderate degree of self-efficacy in being able to discuss issues related to LGBT concerns and issues initially. The material examined through this train-the-trainer program included training style, effective program development and delivery, material on LGBT terminology, transgender issues and concerns on the college campus, and ally development. Although not directly mentioning suicide and mental health, each of these sessions was meant to empower participants to deliver presentations and trainings that would help to change the culture of the university. Through this cultural change, the environmental concerns affecting members of the LGBT community, including isolation, harassment, and violence, can be mediated.

This training was kept small with only ten participants at a time being chosen from applicants. This helped to maintain an open atmosphere where dialogue was encouraged and participants had an opportunity to practice their skills and receive feedback from the trainers. In addition, it allowed for participants to fully embrace the intent of the training, which was to become more self-directed in their learning and style, discuss their experiences (both personal and vicarious), and to understand the real-world application of the material presented. These concepts, all part of adult education theory as presented by Knowles, allow participants to integrate the information into their own experiences and their own lives and work (Lawson, 2010). The material was presented over two days, allowing participants to process the information, live with it, and practice the content as mentioned earlier. In addition, this helped to develop an environment where participants could learn best. It allowed the trainers to minimize lectures; have participants work on projects to gain a better understanding of the material; develop incremental learning opportunities by sectioning information out, referring to workbooks for homework to be done and to help keep participants engaged and on track; and, finally, help the participants understand and develop guides for themselves on how the information may be useful to others and to their jobs. These tips have been identified as the best way to help prevent participants from reaching cognitive overload (Lawson, 2010). In a study of a similar training on cultural competence conducted in a parallel format for pharmacy educators, Assemi, Mutha, and Hudmon (2007) found that the training led to an increased perceived and actual ability to train pharmacy students related to cultural competence. This confirms that these types of programs can have an impact on the diversity self-efficacy of participants.

Other trainings developed were in the format of workshops. These focused on topics related to LGBT adoption, mental health, suicide, campus climate, and retention. While these were conducted across the campus, these were not the sole means for imparting information and training; their foci were on imparting knowledge and increasing sensitivity and awareness. Combs (2002) notes that one of the main reasons trainings related to diversity fail is related to the content and method of delivery. These were supplemental and could be viewed as introductory (prior to the train-the-trainer) or supplemental (continuing education). Trainers from the train-the-trainer program above were able to provide these workshops to students, faculty, and staff across the campus. In all, a total of thirty programs with 450 participants were conducted during the 2010–2011 academic year.

Peer health educators were trained in basic mental health concerns, the mental health continuum, mental health and suicide among college students, mental health and suicide on college campuses, resources, and special populations' mental health and suicide concerns, including LGBT students (see Chapter Four). The peer educators were then asked to serve as change agents for the campus. One such avenue that they used to do this was a vigil held just days after the tragedy of Tyler Clementi's suicide. This brought the entire campus together to discuss bullying and the UNCG campus culture. A total of 300 students, community members, faculty, and staff showed up for the event. In the end, attendees listened to statistics, marched to end violence and bullying, and shared personal stories.

Whereas these trainings focused on stakeholders, these were not necessarily gatekeepers seen on a daily basis by a student or faculty or staff member. These people were not asked to help with developing prevention plans if there was ideation. The people trained through these programs were asked to serve as advocates for the LGBT community and as agents of change in the greater community, and to help decrease stigma of help seeking among LGBT students, faculty, and staff.

Conclusion

As recent media and data related to LGBT suicide indicate, lesbian, gay, bisexual, and transgender students deserve special attention when developing a comprehensive suicide program. However, it is important to note that to develop a successful program, institutions must be aware of campus culture; understand their LGBT community demographics and needs; and develop a working relationship with LGBT students, faculty, and staff. This will help to ensure that the work being done is in conjunction with and being developed for the community and not merely aimed at the community. At UNCG, much of this work had been done with the development of the Safe Zone program in 2000, thus allowing for the development and implementation of the trainings described.

References

American College Health Association. *American College Health Association-National College Health Assessment II: Reference Group Data Report Spring 2010*. Linthicum, Md.: Author, 2010.

Assemi, M., Mutha, S., and Hudmon, K. "Cultural Competence in Pharmacy Education: Evaluation of a Train-the-Trainer Program." *American Journal of Pharmaceutical Education*, 2007, 71(6), 1–8.

Bandura, A. (1994). Self-efficacy. In V. S. Ramachaudran (Ed.), *Encyclopedia of Human Behavior*, vol. 4, pp. 71–81. New York: Academic Press. (Reprinted in H. Friedman [ed.], *Encyclopedia of Mental Health*. San Diego: Academic Press, 1998.)

Beemyn, B. "Serving the Needs of Transgender College Students." *Journal of Gay and Lesbian Issues in Education*, 2003, 1(1), 33–50. doi: 10.1300/J367v01n01_03

Berman, L. "Bullying & Suicide: A Recorded Webinar." American Association of Suicidology Webinar Series, 2010.

Biech, E. *ASTD's Ultimate Train the Trainer: A Complete Guide to Training Success.* Alexandria, Va.: ASTD Press, 2009.

Blanchard, P. N., and Thacker, J. W. *Effective Training: Systems, Strategies, and Practices.* Upper Saddle River, N.J.: Pearson, 2007.

Blumenfeld, W. J., and Cooper, R. M. "LGBT and Allied Youth Responses to Cyberbullying: Policy Implications." *International Journal of Critical Pedagogy*, 2010, 3(1), 114–133.

Bontempo, D. E., and D'Augelli, A. R. "Effects of At-School Victimization and Sexual Orientation on Lesbian, Gay, or Bisexual Youths' Health Risk Behavior." *Journal of Adolescent Health*, 2002, 30(5), 364–374.

Brown, G., Maycock, B., and Burns, S. "Your Picture Is Your Bait: Use and Meaning of Cyberspace Among Gay Men." *Journal of Sex Research*, 2005, 42(1), 63–73.

Carter, K. A. "Transgenderism and College Students: Issues of Gender Identity and Its Role on Our Campuses." In V. A. Wall and N. J. Evans (eds.), *Toward Acceptance: Sexual Orientation Issues on Campus*. Westport, Conn.: Greenwood Press, 2000.

Child Welfare League of America. *The Nation's Children 2009*. Retrieved October 9, 2012, from www.cwla.org/advocacy/nationalfactsheet09.pdf

Clements-Nolle, K., Marx, R., and Katz, M. "Attempted Suicide Among Transgender Persons: The Influence of Gender-Based Discrimination and Victimization." *Journal of Homosexuality*, 2006, 51(3), 53–69.

Combs, G. M. "Meeting the Leadership Challenge of a Diverse and Pluralistic Workplace: Implications of Self-Efficacy for Diversity Training." *Journal of Leadership and Organizational Studies*, 2002, 8(4), 1–16.

D'Augelli, A. R. "Mental Health Problems Among Lesbian, Gay, and Bisexual Youths Ages 14–21." *Clinical Child Psychology and Psychiatry*, 2002, 7, 433–456.

D'Augelli, A. R., Hershberger, S. L., and Pilkington, N. W. "Suicidality Patterns and Sexual Orientation–Related Factors Among Lesbian, Gay, and Bisexual Youths." *Suicide and Life-Threatening Behavior*, 2001, 31(3) 250–264.

Diamond, M. "Sex and Gender Are Different: Sexual Identity and Gender Identity Are Different." *Clinical Child Psychology and Psychiatry*, 2002, 7(3), 320–334.

Egan, J. "Lonely Gay Teen Seeking Same." *New York Times Magazine*, December 10, 2000.

Eisenberg, M. E., and Resnick, M. D. "Suicidality Among Gay, Lesbian and Bisexual Youth: The Role of Protective Factors." *Journal of Adolescent Health*, 2006, 39(5), 662–668.

Ericson, N. "Addressing the Problem of Juvenile Bullying." OJJDP Fact Sheet. U.S. Department of Justice. Office of Juvenile Justice and Delinquency Prevention, June 2001.

Grossman, A. H., and D'Augelli, A. R. "Transgender Youth and Life-Threatening Behaviors." *Suicide and Life-Threatening Behavior*, 2007, 37(5), 527–537.

Heck, N. C., Flentje, A., and Cochran, B. N. "Offsetting Risks: High School Gay-Straight Alliances and Lesbian, Gay, Bisexual, and Transgender (LGBT) Youth." *School Psychology Quarterly*, 2011, 26(2), 161–174.

Herek, G., Chopp, R., and Strohl, D. "Sexual Stigma: Putting Sexual Minority Health Issues in Context." In I. Meyer and M. Northridge (eds.), *The Health of Sexual Minorities: Public Health Perspectives on Lesbian, Gay, Bisexual, and Transgender Populations*. New York: Springer, 2007.

Hillier, L., Kurdas, C., and Horsley, P. *"It's Just Easier": The Internet as a Safety-Net for Same Sex Attracted Young People*. Melbourne: Australian Research Centre in Sex, Health, and Society, Latrobe University, 2001.

Hinduja, S., and Pathcin, J. W. "Cyberbullying: An Exploratory Analysis of Factors Related to Offending and Victimization." *Deviant Behavior*, 2008, 29(2), 129–156.

Igartua, K. J., Gill, K., and Montoro, R. "Internalized Homophobia: A Factor in Depression, Anxiety, and Suicide in the Gay and Lesbian Population." *Canadian Journal of Community Mental Health*, 2003, 22(2), 15–30.

Kidd, S., and others. "The Social Context of Adolescent Suicide Attempts: Interactive Effects of Parent, Peer, and School Social Relations." *Suicide and Life-Threatening Behavior*, 2006, 36(4), 386–395.

Kitts, R. "Gay Adolescents and Suicide: Understanding the Association." *Adolescence*, 2005, 40, 621–628.

Koblin, J. "MySpace: The New Gay Space for Teens and 20-somethings." Columbia News Service, February 14, 2006. Retrieved from http://jscms.jrn.columbia.edu/cns/2006-02-14/koblin-myspace

NEW DIRECTIONS FOR STUDENT SERVICES • DOI: 10.1002/ss

Lawson, K. *The Trainer's Handbook*. San Francisco: Pfeiffer, 2010.

MacDonald, C., and Roberts-Pittman, B. "Cyberbullying Among College Students: Prevalence and Demographic Differences." *Procedia—Social and Behavioral Sciences*, 2010, 9, 2003–2009.

Maczewski, M. "Exploring Identities Through the Internet: Youth Experiences Online." *Child and Youth Care Forum*, 2002, 31(2), 111–129.

McFarlane, M., Bull, S. S., and Rietmeijer, C. A. "Young Adults on the Internet: Risk Behaviors for Sexually Transmitted Diseases and HIV." *Journal of Adolescent Health*, 2002, 31(1), 11–16.

Meyer, I. H. "Minority Stress and Mental Health in Gay Men." *Journal of Health and Social Behavior*, 1995, 36(1), 38–56.

Meyer, I. H. "Prejudice, Social Stress, and Mental Health in Lesbian, Gay, and Bisexual Populations: Conceptual Issues and Research Evidence." *Psychological Bulletin*, 2003, 129(5), 674–697.

Morrow, D. F. "Social Work Practice With Gay, Lesbian, Bisexual, and Transgender Adolescents." *Families in Society*, 2004, 85(1), 91–99.

Nansel T. R., and others. "Bullying Behaviors Among US Youth: Prevalence and Association With Psychosocial Adjustment." *JAMA*, 2001, 285(16), 2094–2100.

Oswalt, S. B., and Wyatt T. J. "Sexual Orientation and Differences in Mental Health, Stress, and Academic Performance in a National Sample of U.S. College Students." *Journal of Homosexuality*, 2011, 58(9), 1255–1280. doi: 10.1080/00918369.2011 .605738

Rankin, S. *Campus Climate for Gay, Lesbian, Bisexual, and Transgender People: A National Perspective*. New York: National Gay and Lesbian Task Force Policy Institute, 2003.

Rankin, S., Blumenfeld, W. J., Weber, G. N., and Frazer, S. *State of Higher Education for Lesbian, Gay, Bisexual, and Transgender People*. Charlotte, N.C.: Campus Pride, 2010.

Rivers, I. "Recollections of Bullying at School and Their Long-Term Implications for Lesbians, Gay Men, and Bisexuals." *Crisis*, 2004, 25(4), 169–175.

Rosario, M., Schrimshaw, E. W., Hunter, J., and Gwadz, M. "Gay-Related Stress and Emotional Distress Among Gay, Lesbian and Bisexual Youths: A Longitudinal Examination." *Journal of Consulting and Clinical Psychology*, 2002, 70(4), 967–975.

Rotheram-Borus, M. J., Hunter, J., and Rosario, M. "Suicidal Behavior and Gay-Related Stress Among Gay and Bisexual Male Adolescents." *Journal of Adolescent Research*, 1994, 9(4), 498–508.

Russell, S. T., and Joyner, K. "Adolescent Sexual Orientation and Suicide Risk: Evidence From a National Study." *American Journal of Public Health*, 2001, 91(8), 1276–1281.

Ryan, C., Huebner, D., Diaz, R. M., and Sanchez, J. "Family Rejection as a Predictor of Negative Health Outcomes in White and Latino Lesbian, Gay, and Bisexual Young Adults." *Pediatrics*, 2009, 123, 346–352.

Safren, S. A., and Heimberg, R. G. "Depression, Hopelessness, Suicidality, and Related Factors in Sexual Minority and Heterosexual Adolescents." *Journal of Consulting and Clinical Psychology*, 1999, 67(6), 859–866.

Suicide Prevention Resource Center. *Suicide Risk and Prevention for Lesbian, Gay, Bisexual, and Transgender Youth*. Newton, Mass.: Education Development Center, 2008.

U.S. Department of Health and Human Services (HHS) Office of the Surgeon General and National Action Alliance for Suicide Prevention. *2012 National Strategy for Suicide Prevention: Goals and Objectives for Action*. Washington, D.C.: HHS, September 2012.

Westefeld, J. S., Maples, M. R., Buford, B., and Taylor, S. (2001). "Gay, Lesbian, and Bisexual College Students: The Relationship Between Sexual Orientation and Depression, Loneliness, and Suicide." *Journal of College Student Psychotherapy*, 2001, *15*, 71–82.

Youth Suicide Prevention Project. "About YSPP." n.d. Retrieved October 9, 2012 from http://www.yspp.org/about_yspp/index.htm

R. BRADLEY JOHNSON is senior assistant director for administrative operations, Department of Housing and Residence Life, at the University of North Carolina at Greensboro.

SYMPHONY OXENDINE is a graduate research assistant in the Higher Education program at the University of North Carolina at Greensboro.

DEBORAH J. TAUB is professor of higher education and coordinator of the Student Personnel Administration in Higher Education program at the University of North Carolina at Greensboro.

JASON ROBERTSON is an assistant professor at Averett University.

NEW DIRECTIONS FOR STUDENT SERVICES • DOI: 10.1002/ss

This chapter presents a brief overview of suicide rates among college students of differing racial, ethnic, ability, and sexual orientation backgrounds in the United States, followed by factors that affect mental health negatively. The chapter concludes with a description of the development of a novel approach to suicide prevention, as implemented at Pace University in New York City.

Suicide Prevention in a Diverse Campus Community

Richard Shadick, Sarah Akhter

As the college population in the United States rapidly diversifies, leaders of successful campus suicide prevention programs are recognizing the importance of targeting specific groups of students. Recent estimates from the National Center for Education Statistics indicated that in 2008 more than one-third (36.7 percent) of college students enrolled in degree-granting institutions were of differing racial, ethnic, and national backgrounds, as compared to just over one-fifth (22.5 percent) in 1990 (Aud, Fox, and KewalRamani, 2010). Students with disabilities are estimated to compose roughly 11 percent of the college population (Raue and Lewis, 2011), whereas between 2 and 5 percent of higher education students identify themselves as nonheterosexual (S. Rankin, personal communication, August 5, 2011).

This chapter presents a brief overview of suicide rates among various groups of students in the United States, followed by factors that negatively affect mental health. The chapter concludes with a description of the development of a novel approach to suicide prevention for a diverse campus, as implemented at Pace University in New York City.

Along with the shifting demographic landscape, colleges continue to face concerns about suicide rates among student populations: 6.2 percent of college students reported seriously considering suicide and 1.3 percent reported attempting suicide at least once within the last year (American

This chapter was developed, in part, under grant number 1U79SM058438-01 from SAMHSA. The views, opinions, and content of this publication are those of the authors and contributors, and do not necessarily reflect the views, opinions, or policies of CMHS, SAMHSA, or HHS, and should not be construed as such.

College Health Association, 2009). Until recently, suicide among college students of varied backgrounds was not a topic under investigation, and professionals seeking guidance in this area were limited to a few studies focused more generally at suicide behavior among persons of color only. Because college constitutes a particular set of developmental opportunities and challenges for traditional-age students (for example, separating from parents) that interact with students' demographic characteristics, the lack of targeted research on suicide behavior in different groups of college students has been problematic for college mental health providers seeking to develop effective suicide prevention programs.

Although comprehensive estimates on suicide behavior among specific groups of college students are lacking, some data derived from large-scale, national, self-report surveys reflect broad group differences. For instance, Brownson and colleagues (forthcoming) investigated suicide behavior in a racially diverse sample of college students using data from a survey conducted by the National Research Consortium of College Counseling Centers in Higher Education (Research Consortium) in 2006 (Drum, Brownson, Burton Denmark, and Smith, 2009). Analyses revealed that non-White students endorsed higher rates of distress and lifetime suicidal ideation and were less likely to seek help for suicide-related distress than White students. More specifically, Alaska Native/American Indian, Asian American, and multiracial and ethnic students endorsed the highest levels of distressed thinking and suicidal thoughts across groups, whereas Black and Latino students endorsed moderate levels of suicidal thoughts.

Similarly, data from the American College Health Association National College Health Assessment Survey (ACHA-NCHA) indicated that Asian American students were 1.6 times more likely to earnestly contemplate suicide than their White peers (Kisch, Leino, and Silverman, 2005) and that 15 percent of American Indian students seriously considered suicide within the past year, with 5.7 percent reporting attempted suicide (Muehlenkamp, Marrone, Gray, and Brown, 2009). Additionally, ACHA-NCHA data revealed higher rates of depression and suicidal ideation among Latinos (Otero, Rivas, and Rivera, 2007).

Despite recent widespread media attention on suicide among gay college students, specific rates of suicidal thoughts or actual deaths are hard to come by in this population. There are, however, data on the likelihood or risk of suicide among sexual minority adolescents derived from the National Longitudinal Study of Adolescent Health (Add Health), which examined health and sexuality in a large, nationally representative sample of adolescents between 1994 and 2008. In their analysis of Add Health data, Russell and Joyner (2001) found a strong link between sexual orientation and suicidal thoughts and behaviors, reporting that adolescents with same-sex attractions were at twice the risk for suicide than their opposite-sex attracted peers. Subsequent analyses of Add Health data also have found a higher prevalence of suicidal tendencies among sexual minority students as compared to their heterosexual peers (Loosier and Dittus, 2010; Silenzio and others, 2007; Teasdale and Bradley-Engen, 2010). If these data generalize to the college population, sexual-minority college students represent a high-risk population.

Related to the risk for suicide among students with disabilities, Svetaz, Ireland, and Blum (2000) used Add Health data to explore emotional distress among adolescents with learning disabilities and found that this group was twice as likely to attempt suicide as their peers without learning disabilities. Confirming this, in a recent meta-review, Giannini and colleagues (2010) reconfirmed that there is an increased risk for suicide among persons with disabilities yet noted that differences exist in suicide rates among persons with different types of disabilities (that is, physical, sensory, cognitive, mental).

Despite the lack of specific and current data on many groups (for example, several racial and ethnic, national, and religious demographics), the available data strongly suggest that some students of differing backgrounds are at higher risk for suicide than their nonminority counterparts. Known factors for suicidality among adolescents include depression, substance abuse, and social conflict (Shaughnessy, Dosi, Jones, and Everett, 2004). Victimization and bullying by peers has also emerged as a cause of suicidal thoughts and behaviors in adolescents (Kaminski and Fang, 2009). Students of differing backgrounds may be subject to bullying by peers based on their perceived differences, whether racial and ethnic, sexual orientation, or ability based. This form of social pressure can become particularly acute in the college setting where students are living independently from their families and must learn to negotiate peer pressures alone. Moreover, college students of varying backgrounds have specific support needs, have reasons why they consider and attempt suicide, and evidence different patterns of seeking help. For instance, a recent investigation found that both stress in dealing with cultural differences and ethnic identity were significant factors in suicidal thoughts among Black students (Walker, Wingate, Obasi, and Joiner, 2008), suggesting that these factors affect members of other groups as well. This diversity and complexity of presentations within the modern college population coupled with the overall heightened risk for suicide among some students of different racial, cultural, sexual, or ability backgrounds result in the imminent need for suicide prevention programs tailored to students of these backgrounds.

Traditionally, suicide prevention in college counseling centers has focused on outreach aimed at raising awareness; providing emergency information (that is, hotlines, counseling center location, crisis procedures) to students, faculty and staff; and brief screening during intake. Literature (that is, pamphlets) is often available in counseling center waiting rooms, listing risk factors, warning signs, and resources; and college counseling center Web sites often feature a page on suicide prevention outlining similar information. Although these efforts do raise awareness, provide emergency resources, and help identify at-risk students, they may not be attuned to the needs of all students. As such, we elected to develop a new approach to suicide prevention specifically aimed at reaching students of varied backgrounds. This approach was designed and implemented at Pace University, a mid-sized liberal arts institution located in lower Manhattan. We begin with a brief description of how we see the impact of diversity on mental health considerations in college students, as our approach to suicide prevention is grounded in this perspective, and then we discuss the process we employed to develop a novel suicide prevention effort.

General Mental Health Considerations for Diverse College Students

As colleges and universities have grown diverse, student affairs professionals are challenged to understand students' multiple identities to be able to meet their needs effectively. Although there are several meaningful aspects of students' identities, based on our college counseling experience, we believe that race, ethnicity, gender, sexual orientation, religion, nationality, and ability level are most directly related to students' mental health. Each of these facets contributes to how students perceive, and are affected by, their world. They are all part of a unique and complex mental health picture and lead to decisions in seeking help when a student is in need.

These core identities also have implications for how a student is perceived and treated by others on and off campus. For example, acts of prejudice can significantly affect a student's mental health. Microaggressions, discrimination, and hate crimes take place with disturbing frequency on campuses. If they are chronic, intense, and occur in the absence of social supports, these acts can result in deleterious effects on academic, social, and emotional functioning. Microaggressions are brief and commonplace daily verbal, behavioral, and environmental indignities, whether intentional or unintentional, that communicate hostile, derogatory, or negative cultural slights and insults to the target person or group. Although they may be more subtle than an act of discrimination or a hate crime, microaggressions do lead to stress (Sue and others, 2007). Discrimination is the unlawful and intentional act of unfair treatment of a person based on race, ethnicity, gender, religion, national origin, physical or mental disability, and age. Discrimination, because of its overt nature, may have a more obvious or immediate impact on students than microaggressions. Hate crimes are those that manifest prejudice based on race, religion, sexual orientation, disability, or ethnicity (Federal Hate Crimes Statistics Act, 1990) and have the most immediate, deleterious effects on student mental health. Although not definite outcomes, depression, anxiety, or posttraumatic stress may occur.

Negative mental health is not a consistent outcome when an individual is exposed to some forms of prejudice, and in fact some argue that discrimination fosters greater resilience and social cohesion (Arrington and Wilson, 2000). However, the Minority Stress Model (Meyer, 1995) predicted that negative mental health outcomes occur as a result of prejudice. Meyer (1995) used homophobia experienced by lesbian and gay individuals to illustrate how minority stressors, including internalized homophobia, stigma, and prejudice, lead to psychic distress (such as demoralization, guilt, suicide ideation, poor health). Meyer (2003) and (Balsam and others (2011) also make the case that, if an individual has multiple diverse identities (for example, a disabled Asian lesbian), then the likelihood, intensity, and frequency of discrimination increases.

In cases where an individual has been exposed to severe or widespread discrimination, the likelihood of need for support is higher. With individuals of differing backgrounds, research has demonstrated that attitudes toward seeking help may hinder accessing services (Brownson and others, forthcoming) such that individuals are less likely to ask for help if they anticipate that their efforts will lead to misunderstanding of who they are, what they experience, or a sense of stigma. Additionally, students are less likely to get help if they are confronted with a health or mental health care staff that does not mirror their own racial diversity (Townes, Chavez-Korell, and Cunningham, 2009.)

Pace University Suicide Prevention

Hesitance of students to seek services due to fear of stigma or being misunderstood can be a significant hindrance to preventing suicide. Without attention to this, developing and implementing suicide prevention programs can be stymied. Thus, in designing a suicide prevention plan targeting students from differing backgrounds, we first chose to conduct extensive research prior to soliciting direct input from students. We focused our research efforts on the seven campus populations that were neglected in the suicide prevention literature but that had a significant presence on the Pace University campus: African American; Asian American; Latino; lesbian, gay, bisexual, and questioning (LGBQ); international; Muslim; and disabled students.

During the research phase, we conducted an extensive literature review in the psychological and social science fields. In addition to journals, books, and dissertations, we also included printed material and diversity-oriented Web sites in our review to ensure a sampling of information and programs not published. Additional information was obtained from expert resources in the field such as the Suicide Prevention Resource Center, the American Association of Suicidology, and by fellow Garret Lee Smith Memorial grantee programs. Finally, we also studied data derived from studies in which Pace University participated, including the Research Consortium (Drum, Brownson, Burton Denmark, and Smith, 2009) and the

Center for College Student Mental Health (Castonguay, Locke, and Hayes, 2011).

With the research phase complete, our next step was to talk directly with students about their experiences of depression, suicide, and counseling in a focus-group format. However, one of the most important discoveries we made during our research was that students from different backgrounds often attribute vastly different meanings and emotions to depression, suicide, and counseling. We realized that taking steps to be knowledgeable about these variations but also being open to new discoveries would be imperative to overcome student wariness about discussing sensitive issues. We were also keenly aware of factors that could hinder students from accessing mental health services, including historical or cultural influences and the stigma of seeking mental health services, and realized that these same factors might cause students to avoid participation in our focus groups. As predicted, initial focus groups run at the counseling center did not draw students, even when food and incentives were offered. Instead, we realized it was essential for us to go to the students—in classrooms, clubs and organizations, and residence halls. We also reached out to student leaders, peer leaders, and other active students, and asked faculty and administrators for help with recruitment. We found that students were more likely to talk with us if they were referred by a trusted friend, community member, or mentor.

Once focus groups were up and running, we noticed that language played an important role in how much students shared. For instance, terms such as *mental illness*, *depression*, and *suicide* connote negative concepts of weakness and disturbance. Additionally, words were not universal and some concepts were simply not present in some languages or cultures and disdained in others. Rather than alienate our students with the language we used, we asked them to label and identify the concepts of interest for us. To address these issues, it was essential to show interest, respect, and a genuine curiosity of the students' experiences. Appreciative inquiry (AI; Boyd and Bright, 2007; Cooperrider, Whitney, and Stavros, 2003) offered a viable method to accessing students' experiences. AI is a method of understanding a person, group, or system by asking questions about strengths and positive characteristics rather than focusing on problems or conflicts. We found AI to be quite helpful in collecting data as well as in demonstrating to students that the counseling center is sensitive to differing needs.

Our research and focus group data revealed that classic suicide prevention strategies (based primarily on White populations) miss key signs and symptoms of different populations. Thus, we tailored our prevention strategies to reflect the culture-specific symptoms our students had discussed with us. For example, some Latino students referenced *ataques de nervios* (sudden panic attack–like episodes that can involve brief yet intense externalizing or somatic symptoms) and noted how this could play a role in a crisis leading to suicide. Some Asian students were more likely to describe physical symptoms of their stress, such as concerns like headaches, stomachaches, and backaches, than to endorse traditional symptoms of depression or anxiety. This has obvious implications for where they present to get help; they are more likely to go to a health care unit than a counseling center.

The focus group discussions also reinforced our understanding that family, religion, and broader cultural factors affect suicide-related behaviors. Serving as protective factors, families, religious institutions, and communities can prevent suicide among at-risk individuals by providing much needed support in times of trouble. Additionally, these social institutions often discourage the act of taking one's life. For example, Catholic countries in South America have some of the lowest rates of suicide in the world because suicide is seen as a sin. However, instead of serving as preventative factors, in other instances these institutions may not value, or actively discourage, discussing familial or personal concerns with strangers (that is, mental health providers) out of distrust, fear, or sense of privacy. For some groups, historic events (for example, the Tuskegee experiments) have reinforced distrust of the mental health field with its ties to medicine. One of the more universal values our students shared with us was that discussing personal problems outside of the family can be an act of betrayal. In the international population, some of the students came from locales that simply do not have, or believe in, mental health services. Moreover, the above factors can exacerbate the common anxieties experienced by many students who access service: fear of jeopardizing their academic standing, losing their housing, or disappointing their families by disclosing suicidality.

In some cases, our focus groups found there to be circumstances where suicide was encouraged. Traditional, rural cultures in and around India and Pakistan, despite governmental prohibitions, sometimes encourage suicide when a shameful event such as rape or infidelity occurs. In other Asian countries suicide is an "acceptable" way to handle other shameful circumstances that may dishonor the family. Some students, simply by coming from countries that have higher rates of suicide death (for example, some northern European countries), may view suicide as a societally approved manner of dealing with one's feelings.

To further enhance our understanding, we also solicited information on mental health issues among our students of differing backgrounds from faculty and staff. We felt they offered a valuable perspective as they were on the front lines in the defense against suicide. Their feedback illustrated the many different ways they struggled to get students the support they need either through the counseling center, their spiritual community, or family. It also became evident that faculty and staff often had a narrow, western European view of mental health, and this had implications for the outreach that needed to occur to ensure they identified mental health problems in students and made appropriate referrals.

New Directions for Student Services • DOI: 10.1002/ss

In sum, our research, focus groups, and conversations with faculty and staff provided us with a wealth of information on suicide-relevant issues among our students. The next task was to develop a suicide prevention program based on what we had learned. It quickly became evident that true expertise on each student subpopulation was not possible and that the information we had amassed needed to be organized strategically. Our solution was to glean general concepts about the key differences of diverse student groups and then use them for our consultation and outreach efforts to the student body as a whole.

Recommendations for Suicide Prevention in College Students from Differing Backgrounds

Synthesis of our data resulted in the development of a suicide prevention kit, featuring a PowerPoint presentation on multicultural suicide prevention. The presentation covered a discussion of multiculturalism; the impact microaggressions, discrimination, and hate crimes have on mental health; and signs and symptoms of suicide in eight campus populations (African American, Asian American, Latino, Caucasian, LGBQ, international, Muslim, and disabled students). The presentation also provided guidance on how to make a referral that takes into account each student's background. Accompanying brochures, a poster, fact sheets, self-study quizzes, role-plays, and bibliographies were included in the kit for each of the diverse student groups. Individual brochures were developed for each of the student groups, focusing on unique signs, symptoms, and risk factors and providing suggestions for making culturally sensitive referrals. The poster was used as a way to attract interest on the topic of suicide prevention for students by listing a fact on each of the seven groups and contact information of the counseling center. The brochure and posters used eye-catching artwork, which subsequently led to many on campus displaying them. (A copy of these, as well as the rest of the kit, can be found at www.pace.edu /counseling/). Fact sheets were developed to highlight the main points from the research we completed on each of the student groups. Role-plays and quizzes were also developed to help users of the kit interact and learn more of the material. Finally, bibliographies for the student groups were included if users wished to learn more.

A decision was made to develop the PowerPoint presentation and supporting material in a manner that was easily tailored to other institutions' needs. Once completed, all the materials were posted on the Pace University Counseling Center Web site and the kit was listed in the Suicide Prevention Resource Center's Best Practices Registry so that others could learn of and access the material. To date the kit has been disseminated to 300 colleges, universities, mental health, and community centers. Plans are under way to assess how the material was used, how helpful it was, and to determine what changes were made when institutions used it on their own campus.

Drum, Brownson, Burton Denmark, and Smith (2009) found that students are more likely to turn to peers than to a professor, clergy, or mental health provider when in a suicidal crisis. With this in mind, in addition to the usual suicide prevention trainings for faculty and staff, we offered our multicultural suicide prevention trainings to the boards of student clubs and organizations, peer leaders of orientation classes for first-year students, and residence hall advisers. Based on our knowledge that students tend to seek services after hours, we realized that Web-based prevention approaches would be helpful. In addition to providing dynamic Web sites that offer information in an engaging fashion, we used an online screening tool hosted by the Jed Foundation. (The American Association of Suicidology also offers an online screening program for students with live follow up from a clinician.) These methods of outreach can be an effective means of connecting with students (Haas and others, 2008), particularly for those who are averse to setting foot in a counseling center or health service.

Although it is important to reach all students on campus, prevention efforts should target at-risk or vulnerable populations. As noted earlier, it is impossible to provide prevention that is tailored to every group; however, some populations, either due to a sudden negative campus event (for example, a high-profile student suicide surrounding a hate crime) or long-standing discrimination on campus, should be reached out to. As noted earlier, there are elevated rates of suicidal thoughts for differing student groups (Brownson and others, forthcoming). We chose our seven groups after our analysis of our data from focus groups and assessments. These rates vary from campus to campus; thus, assessment is needed to identify key student groups. Focus groups of key campus constituents are helpful. Participation in various research studies that assess mental health trends on campus is another way. Studies organized by the Research Consortium (Drum, Brownson, Burton Denmark, and Smith, 2009), the Center for College Student Mental Health (Castonguay, Locke, and Hayes, 2011), and the American College Health Assessment (American College Health Association, 2009) are relatively easy and inexpensive ways to obtain a sense of the mental health on a campus. These studies also provide an opportunity to compare campus trends with national averages so that suicide prevention planning can take place.

The traditional methods of prevention we have used in the past have included putting up posters, passing out brochures at cafeteria tables and suicide prevention events, placing public service announcements on the university radio station and on campus video screens, putting flyers in student mailboxes, and programming in the residence halls. However, these passive prevention efforts aimed at promoting mental health among college students have had limited efficacy (Fountoulakis, Gonda, and Rihmer, 2011). Our research has found that a community approach that is active and engaging, university-wide, and sustained is more likely to engage our student population, bring in students who need help, decrease hospitalizations, and reduce the likelihood of suicide attempts. Data from our multicultural suicide prevention workshops have indicated that 80 percent of attendees have found the information useful and that 100 percent would use it in their daily lives to prevent suicide. Our prevention efforts have led to multiyear, double-digit increases in the use of counseling center services (prior to implementing the program we had more modest increases), which has led to many more suicidal students getting help and the absence of suicide death on campus.

References

American College Health Association. "National College Health Assessment Spring 2008 Reference Group Data Report (abridged): The American College Health Association." *Journal of American College Health*, 2009, 57(5), 477–488.

Arrington, E., and Wilson, M. "A Re-examination of Risk and Resilience During Adolescence: Incorporating Culture and Diversity." *Journal of Child and Family Studies*, 2000, 9(2), 221–230.

Aud, S., Fox, M., and KewalRamani, A. *Status and Trends in the Education of Racial and Ethnic Groups*. U.S. Department of Education, National Center for Education Statistics. Washington, D.C.: U.S. Government Printing Office, 2010. (NCES 2010-015.)

Balsam, K. F., and others. "Measuring Multiple Minority Stress: The LGBT People of Color Microaggressions Scale." *Cultural Diversity and Ethnic Minority Psychology*, 2011, 17(2), 163–174.

Boyd, N. M., and Bright, D. S. "Appreciative Inquiry as a Mode of Action Research for Community Psychology." *Journal of Community Psychology*, 2007, 35(8), 1019–1036.

Brownson, C., and others. "Suicidal Behavior and Help Seeking in College Student Racial and Ethnic Groups." *Journal of College Counseling*, forthcoming.

Castonguay, L. G., Locke, B. D., and Hayes, J. A. "The Center for Collegiate Mental Health: An Example of a Practice-Research Network in University Counseling Centers." *Journal of College Student Psychotherapy*, 2011, 25(2), 105–119.

Cooperrider, D. L., Whitney, D., and Stavros, J. M. *Appreciative Inquiry Handbook: The First in a Series of AI Workbooks for Leaders of Change*. Bedford Heights, Ohio: Lakeshore Communications, 2003.

Drum, D. J., Brownson, C., Burton Denmark, A., and Smith, S. E. "New Data on the Nature of Suicidal Crises in College Students: Shifting the Paradigm." *Professional Psychology: Research and Practice*, 2009, 40(3), 213–222.

Federal Hate Crimes Statistics Act. 28 U.S.C. S. 534, 1990.

Fountoulakis, K. N., Gonda, X., and Rihmer, Z. "Suicide Prevention Programs Through Community Intervention." *Journal of Affective Disorders*, 2011, 130, 10–16.

Giannini, M. J., and others. "Understanding Suicide and Disability Through Three Major Disabling Conditions: Intellectual Disability, Spinal Cord Injury, and Multiple Sclerosis." *Disability and Health Journal*, 2010, 3, 74–78.

Haas, A., and others. "An Interactive Web-Based Method of Outreach to College Students at Risk for Suicide." *Journal of American College Health*, 2008, 57(1), 15–22.

Kaminski, J., and Fang, X. "Victimization by Peers and Adolescent Suicide in Three U.S. Samples." *The Journal of Pediatrics*, 2009, 155(5), 683–688.

Kisch, J., Leino, E. V., and Silverman, M. M. "Aspects of Suicidal Behavior, Depression, and Treatment in College Students: Results From the Spring 2000 National College Health Assessment Survey." *Suicide and Life-Threatening Behavior,* 2005, *35*(1), 3–13.

Loosier, P. S., and Dittus, P. J. "Group differences in risk across three domains using an expanded measure of sexual orientation." *Journal of Primary Prevention,* 2010, *31*(5–6), 261–272.

Meyer, I. "Minority Stress and Mental Health in Gay Men." *Journal of Health and Social Behavior,* 1995, *36*(1), 38–56.

Meyer, I. H. "Prejudice, Social Stress, and Mental Health in Lesbian, Gay and Bisexual Populations: Conceptual Issues and Research Evidence." *Psychological Bulletin,* 2003, *129*, 674–697.

Muehlenkamp, J. J., Marrone, S., Gray, J. S., and Brown, D. L. "A College Suicide Prevention Model for American Indian Students." *Professional Psychology: Research and Practice,* 2009, *40*(2), 134–140.

Otero, R., Rivas, O., and Rivera, R. "Predicting Persistence of Hispanic Students in Their 1st Year of College." *Journal of Hispanic Higher Education,* 2007, *6*, 163–173.

Raue, K., and Lewis, L. *Students With Disabilities at Degree-Granting Postsecondary Institutions.* U.S. Department of Education, National Center for Education Statistics. Washington, D.C.: U.S. Government Printing Office, 2011. (NCES 2011–018.)

Russell, S. T., and Joyner, K. "Adolescent Sexual Orientation and Suicide Risk: Evidence From a National Study." *American Journal of Public Health,* 2001, *91*(8), 1276–1281.

Shaughnessy, L., Dosi, S., Jones, S., and Everett, S. "Attempted Suicide and Associated Health-Risk Behaviors among Native American High School Students." *Journal of School Health,* 2004, *74*(5), 177–182.

Silenzio, V. M. B., and others. "Sexual Orientation and Risk Factors for Suicidal Ideation and Suicide Attempts Among Adolescents and Young Adults." *American Journal of Public Health,* 2007, *97*(11), 2017–2019.

Sue, D. W., and others. "Racial Microaggressions in Everyday Life: Implications for Clinical Practice." *American Psychologist,* 2007, *62*(4), 271–286.

Svetaz, M. V., Ireland, M., and Blum, R. "Adolescents With Learning Disabilities: Risk and Protective Factors Associated With Emotional Well-Being: Findings From the National Longitudinal Study of Adolescent Health." *Journal of Adolescent Health,* 2000, *27*(5), 340–348.

Teasdale, B., and Bradley-Engen, M. "Adolescent Same-Sex Attraction and Mental Health: The Role of Stress and Support." *Journal of Homosexuality,* 2010, *57*(2), 287–309.

Townes, D. L., Chavez-Korell, S., and Cunningham, N. J. "Reexamining the Relationships Between Racial Identity, Cultural Mistrust, Help-Seeking Attitudes, and Preference for a Black Counselor." *Journal of Counseling Psychology,* 2009, *56*(2), 330–336.

Walker, R. L., Wingate, L. R., Obasi, E. M., and Joiner, T. E., Jr. "An Empirical Investigation of Acculturative Stress and Ethnic Identity as Moderators for Depression and Suicidal Ideation in College Students." *Cultural Diversity and Ethnic Minority Psychology,* 2008, *14*(1), 75–82.

RICHARD SHADICK *is director of the Pace University Counseling Center.*

SARAH AKHTER *is staff psychologist at the Pace University Counseling Center.*

This chapter explores activities and processes typically used after a suicide event as a prevention strategy to address suicide on campus. Special issues in postsuicide intervention and suggestions for development of appropriate protocols are highlighted.

Postsuicide Intervention as a Prevention Tool: Developing a Comprehensive Campus Response to Suicide and Related Risk

M. Dolores Cimini, Estela M. Rivero

Introduction

This chapter explores the critical role of crisis intervention and other support after a suicide has occurred as part of a comprehensive suicide prevention response within college and university campuses. The important components of postsuicide intervention campus crisis response and protocols and the identification of key stakeholders to implement these protocols are discussed. Special issues in postsuicide intervention, such as the role of social media, working with campus media, considerations associated with the planning of memorials, and self-care for responders to a student suicide, are explored. Finally, the importance of planning a coordinated and collaborative campus response prior to the onset of a campus crisis and ongoing evaluation of the effectiveness of such a response are outlined.

Why Is Postsuicide Intervention Important?

Risk for suicide among college students is a major public health issue that affects institutions of higher education across the nation. Research indicates that the rate for suicide among college students is believed to be in the neighborhood of seven or eight suicides per 100,000 students (Drum, Brownson, Burton Denmark, and Smith, 2009; Garlow and others, 2008; Haas and others, 2008). Despite research indicating that suicide among college students is infrequent, completed suicides do occur, and such tragic events affect the student's family, his or her peers, and the campus community as a whole. For this reason, colleges and universities must be prepared to respond to the devastating effects of suicide through crisis response and postsuicide intervention efforts delivered to individuals and families and within the broader campus environment.

Postsuicide intervention has been defined in a number of ways in the suicide prevention literature. The Suicide Prevention Resource Center workgroup (2008) defines postsuicide intervention as "the provision of crisis intervention and other support after a suicide has occurred to address and alleviate possible effects of suicide." Meilman and Hall (2006) indicate that postsuicide intervention efforts are ". . . interventions occurring after a tragedy." Although each of the above definitions of postsuicide intervention focuses on a slightly different perspective, each underscores the need to develop and offer services to those directly affected by a student suicide.

Equally important are the aims of postsuicide intervention efforts to prevent further loss of life and reduce the severity of potential mental health issues that might arise subsequent to a student suicide. Thus, postsuicide intervention efforts exist hand in hand with crisis response activities, and the postsuicide intervention process, in turn, informs future prevention and intervention efforts. To reach the broadest segment of the institution through postsuicide intervention work, both crisis response and postsuicide intervention must be viewed within a comprehensive framework that reaches individuals and groups at multiple intervention points and is delivered in a coordinated, collaborative, responsive, and proactive manner.

The Role of Postsuicide Intervention Within a Comprehensive Campus Suicide Prevention Framework

Addressing health risk behaviors using a comprehensive prevention framework is a familiar concept to many student affairs administrators and prevention practitioners. In its landmark document addressing alcohol use among college students, the Task Force on College Drinking of the National Institute on Alcohol Abuse and Alcoholism (2002) indicated that comprehensive prevention efforts should use a "3-in-1 Framework;" that is, efforts must be able to reach individual students who may be at risk, the student body as a whole, and the college or university campus and surrounding community.

The public health approach to prevention defines comprehensive prevention activities as occurring simultaneously at multiple levels: with the entire campus community (universal prevention), with students at risk (early intervention), and with students who have already developed problems requiring treatment and referral (specialized prevention). More specifically, within a comprehensive suicide prevention and postsuicide

Figure 7.1. Spectrum of Intervention Response: Suicide Prevention

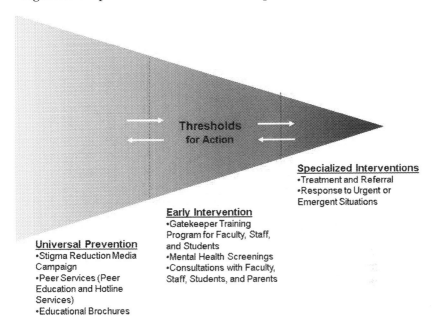

intervention model, universal strategies might include social marketing campaigns and brochure dissemination; early interventions might include mental health screenings and gatekeeper training programs; and specialized interventions might include counseling services, referral for medication treatment, and responding to urgent or emergent mental health concerns on campus (see Figure 7.1).

In the preceding framework, comprehensive prevention activities take place in the context of a feedback loop. Each key element delivered across the prevention spectrum connects with the others under the umbrella of an overarching set of goals and objectives. The evaluation of each component informs the implementation of future prevention strategies or modifications of existing strategies.

The death of a student through suicide on a college campus often triggers a review of the institution's existing prevention and intervention services and programs. Suicides can lead to the evaluation, modification, or addition of prevention efforts. The existence of a comprehensive crisis response and postsuicide intervention protocol, therefore, not only guides the actions of a college or university in the aftermath of a student death, but also informs the refinement of prevention efforts at all levels. The important task of postsuicide intervention protocol development, therefore, requires a thoughtful, deliberate and strategic process that involves key stakeholders representing a broad spectrum of constituencies within the institution.

Development of Postsuicide Intervention Protocols

Key considerations associated with crisis response and postsuicide intervention protocol development include the identification of stakeholders to make up a crisis response and postsuicide intervention team and the development of postsuicide intervention guidelines that meet campus needs. The first step in this process is selecting a broad base of campus and community representatives, who will inform the development of the protocol and, during a crisis, will support and guide its implementation. These stakeholders may include university administrators; student affairs staff members; and students working in paraprofessional capacities within the institution, such as student ambulance personnel. In addition, it is helpful to include representatives from the campus police department, division of academic affairs, and media relations office. Finally, community representatives, including staff members from the local police department, hospital, and psychiatric center can play an important role in the development of postsuicide intervention protocols.

A campus crisis response and postsuicide intervention team must include a representative from the campus counseling center or, when there is no campus counseling center, a psychological consultant to ensure that all elements of the response process address the many complex mental health issues that may arise after a suicide. Figure 7.2 provides an example of a crisis response and postsuicide intervention team roster for a college or university setting.

After the crisis response and postsuicide intervention team is assembled, members should outline and document procedures, describing clearly how the campus will provide support and assistance to students in crisis and enhance their safety and the safety of others. The members of the crisis response and postsuicide intervention team also should clarify institutional responses, as confidentiality regulations permit, to persons or groups such as the student's parents, legal guardians, or significant others; the student's friends, roommates, suitemates, hall residents; various institutional offices providing services and support to affected students and other affected members of the university community; and, when appropriate, the community beyond the college or university.

During the development of postsuicide intervention protocols, team members must consider and address system-wide process issues that could affect efficient implementation of the protocols during a time of crisis. These include the manner in which members of the college or university will address confidentiality issues; how decisions will be made and who

Figure 7.2. Listing of Crisis Response and Postsuicide Intervention Team Representatives on a College or University Campus

College/University Representatives

- Academic Support Services
- Campus Media Relations Office
- Campus Ministry
- Counseling Services
- Disability Resource Center
- Facilities/Physical Plant
- Financial Aid
- Graduate Studies
- Health Center
- International Student Services
- Judicial Affairs
- Police Department
- Residential Life
- Student Life
- Undergraduate Studies
- Vice President for Student Affairs
- Vice President for Academic Affairs
- Student Service Groups:
  o Campus Ambulance Service
  o Campus Peer Education Program

Community Representatives

- Fire Department
- Police Department
- Hospital/Emergency Room
- Psychiatric Center
- Mobile Mental Health Crisis Intervention Team (if applicable)

will make them; how communication will take place; and how support will be offered, both to responders and to students and other members of the campus community.

Confidentiality. University staff members who respond to crises must be aware that students have a right to privacy and that, in some instances, they might not wish to have information shared with others. At the same time, there are situations in which the release of information is permissible and necessary. For example, information should be disclosed to appropriate individuals in connection with an emergency when the knowledge of such information is necessary to protect the health or safety of the student or other individuals. In situations where immediate threats to health and safety are not present, the need to release information without the permission of the student is less clear. In such cases, university

NEW DIRECTIONS FOR STUDENT SERVICES • DOI: 10.1002/ss

leadership, including legal counsel, should be consulted. In any situation, it is prudent to attempt to obtain the student's permission to release information.

Different university records are subject to different standards of confidentiality. For example, counseling records are subject to stricter standards of confidentiality under state laws than many other kinds of records. In general, however, student counseling records should not be released without the written permission of the individual to whom the record pertains. There are a few exceptions to this principle; most notably, as mentioned above, records may be released to appropriate persons and entities when necessary to prevent serious harm to the client or another individual.

Judgment. Any staff member involved in a crisis at a college or university should aim to use his or her own best judgment regarding how to respond. What constitutes "best judgment" is best considered within the context of an institution's policies, practices, regulations, and expectations. In general, however, key elements to consider might include which issues require immediate action, what else should be done for the student(s) in crisis, who else might be affected and what support is available for them, and who should be notified with what types of information. Although these issues must be clarified quickly in an emergency, professionals on the crisis intervention and postsuicide intervention team or administrative or supervisory staff should be consulted.

Coordination. Prevention, crisis intervention, and postsuicide intervention involve a number of different units of a college or university that typically communicate with one another and share responsibility for intervening and deciding whom else to involve. The dean or vice president for student affairs coordinates notification and crisis intervention services on many campuses, but specific institutional needs might dictate that other offices are appropriate for coordination of these efforts.

Coordination of services involves a number of steps, including assessing the situation, with particular attention to the nature and extent of the crisis; identifying person(s) who need support; determining who will provide direct and indirect services; informing appropriate individuals and offices of the situation; following up with individuals and offices about what action should be taken; following up to assess the impact of interventions; and determining whether future action is necessary.

In addition, postsuicide intervention and crisis responses should be reviewed within one or two weeks of the crisis and a month or more after the crisis, to examine the effect of the response. Persons who were involved in responding to the crisis, including all back-up and support service representatives, should be involved in these reviews. Individuals and groups affected by the crisis also should be invited to provide feedback regarding the crisis response. The scheduling of the interim and longer-term postsuicide intervention reviews should be guided by the circumstances

NEW DIRECTIONS FOR STUDENT SERVICES • DOI: 10.1002/ss

surrounding the particular crisis event, as the response that is most appropriate for each crisis situation is as unique as the response being executed and evaluated.

Support. Support for students in crisis subsequent to the suicide of a peer or other serious life event may be provided in a number of ways. For example, students in crisis might benefit from personal, academic, or financial support. Because students in crisis might be particularly receptive to intervention, staff members should use this opportunity to help the students learn from their experiences. Responsibility for providing support can be shared among staff members, family, friends, and other individuals. As part of a broad-based umbrella of support, a student can be referred to services such as the campus counseling center, the academic dean, office of financial aid, and other college and university departments as appropriate.

A number of specific and helpful response alternatives are available to faculty members to support students in crisis. These include recommending psychological counseling services; extending a deadline; offering special tutoring, make-up work, or examinations; excluding one or more test grades from the final grade computation; computing the final grade or class standing without all work being completed; or facilitating a leave of absence or medical withdrawal. In the event of financial crisis, student or institutional financial services might be able to assist by suggesting whom to notify to alter payment schedules, receive emergency funds, or facilitate other arrangements.

Special Issues in Postsuicide Intervention

Attempts to address risk behaviors or crisis situations are likely to encounter issues and challenges at the individual, environmental, and system levels. For example, while counseling services staff meet with groups of bereaved friends after a suicide, academic and student administrators work with family of the deceased student to plan a memorial service, and the campus external relations office responds to requests from local media for details about the student suicide and the institution's response to it. Such a complex set of circumstances calls for the planning and execution of crisis response and postsuicide intervention efforts with a comprehensive framework in mind. That is, as the myriad consequences of the suicide are addressed, prevention strategies to help the campus and its members heal from the tragedy and move forward also must be created. This task often begins by systematically moving outward from the initial focus of the crisis situation—that is, the deceased student—and identifying the family members, friends, peers, classmates, advisers, employers, and other key individuals connected to the deceased student. As affected individuals and groups are identified over the hours, days, and weeks after a suicide, the crisis response and postsuicide intervention team can plan methods of reaching out to these individuals in a manner that is relevant and responsive to the needs of each group. This might include telephone calls, e-mail messages, residence hall and classroom meetings, and other types of contacts.

Interventions made with individuals and groups associated with the deceased student usually must have a broad reach. A number of special issues arise, however, when considering a broad institutional response to student suicide across environmental and system levels. These include the role of social networking after a suicide, the planning of memorial services, working with campus media, and self-care for responders. The following paragraphs address each of these issues.

Social Media and Postsuicide Intervention. When someone dies by suicide, that individual's online social media profile often becomes a central point for friends and family to talk about the suicide and memorialize the individual who died. Exposure to suicide, whether through a family member, peer, or other personal connection, or through figures in the media, is an established risk factor for suicide. There is substantial evidence that certain messages (for example, those that glamorize the suicide) and certain information (for example, details regarding the method of suicide used) may contribute to the occurrence of multiple suicides within a short time frame, and can increase risk of such an occurrence.

When implementing crisis response and postsuicide intervention strategies in a college or university setting, the role of the Internet must be considered so that postsuicide intervention initiatives target existing online communities. This is especially important when the deceased individual is between the ages of 15 and 24, the age range of most college students in the United States, as data indicate this age group is very active online (National Suicide Prevention Lifeline, 2010). As a result, those individuals who would most be affected by the suicide might be connected to the deceased student and others via online social networking sites (for example, Facebook, Twitter) and might be engaging in online conversation about the suicide very soon after it occurs. Such an online presence by college students offers college or university staff members conducting crisis response and postsuicide intervention efforts an important and efficient means of distributing information and resources, as well as of monitoring students and other individuals connected to the deceased student for any indications of suicide risk.

In brief, the postsuicide intervention work done in "real-world" communities should be replicated online. Comprehensive crisis response and postsuicide intervention strategies, when applied to online environments, will assist those affected by a suicide within higher education settings, in addition to using social media sites to further these efforts. The National Suicide Prevention Lifeline (2010) recommends that college or university staff members coordinating crisis response and postsuicide intervention initiatives use social networking sites to distribute relevant information and resources and monitor comments from individuals connected to the bereaved students. Furthermore, those overseeing these efforts should collaborate with parents and family members of the deceased student to ensure that they monitor their student's social media sites that remain available online subsequent to the student's death. Crisis responders also should work with families of the deceased student to bypass any privacy settings that would prohibit the activities outlined above.

Conducting Memorial Services. Public communication after a suicide can affect the suicide risk of those receiving the communication (Centers for Disease Control, 2001). Some types of communication about the deceased and his or her actions may influence others to imitate or model the suicidal behavior. Therefore, it is important not to glamorize the current state of "peace" the deceased may have found through death. Although some religious perspectives consider the afterlife to be much better than life in the physical realm, this contrast should not be overemphasized in a public gathering. If there are others in the audience who are dealing with psychological pain or suicidal thoughts, the lure of finding peace or escape through death might add to the attractiveness of suicide. Information about resources for treatment and support should be made available to those attending the observance. In a similar way, one should avoid normalizing the suicide by interpreting it as a reasonable response to particularly distressing life circumstances.

Instead, a clear distinction, even separation, should be made between the positive accomplishments and qualities of the deceased student and his or her final act. Make the observation that, although the deceased student is no longer suffering or in turmoil, we would prefer she or he had lived in a society that understood those who suffer from mental or behavioral health problems and supported those who seek help for those problems without a trace of stigma or prejudice.

In the case of multiple suicides or "suicide clusters" occurring on a college or university campus, all memorial responses should be conducted in an equitable manner, taking into consideration the unique personal, religious, familial, and other factors associated with each situation. Environmental or system factors, such as the time point during the academic year in which each suicide takes place, should be considered. The response to each suicide should be as unique as the individual student and network that are affected.

Working with Campus Media. At many colleges and universities, the campus media, or external relations, office serves as the information gateway to communities outside the campus. For this reason, a representative from the campus media office should be included in the crisis response and postsuicide intervention team so accurate communications, based on known facts and knowledge from mental health experts on campus, are disseminated. Colleagues from campus media relations offices also should be prepared to address tragedies such as student suicides before they occur. For example, media-specific response protocols may be developed, and members of the campus postsuicide intervention response team may be designated in advance as experts or spokespersons for the institution. Staff members from the counseling center and health services can prepare a list of talking points about suicide and the postsuicide intervention responses taking place on a campus. All these steps, if completed in preparation for the potential occurrence of a campus tragedy, can ease the challenges of addressing external inquiries quickly and thoroughly when a crisis does occur.

Campus media staff also should recognize that some reporters may penetrate campus or college student social networking sites to access contact information of the friends and family of the deceased student. Peer educators or student ambulance personnel, particularly those whose work focuses on the prevention of suicide, might be contacted by reporters for comment as well. In these cases, members of the campus community, particularly those most directly involved in a response to a student suicide, should know that they must notify the campus media office if they receive any outside media requests.

Self-Care for Responders. Ensuring the opportunity for self-care for responders subsequent to a student suicide is a critical dimension to address within a crisis response and postsuicide intervention protocol. Responders may have a number of reactions after a suicide. For example, if staff members or students had contact with the body of the deceased student, they might be traumatized by this and might require immediate psychological intervention. The death of a student through suicide might trigger reactions of grief related to the recent or past loss of loved ones. In cases in which a responder has a psychiatric diagnosis of depression, anxiety, posttraumatic stress disorder, or other condition, that condition might be exacerbated. Responding to a suicide might also trigger the initial onset of a psychiatric condition in a responder. In addition, college or university administrators, peers, or counseling center staff members might question their own responses after the fact and wonder whether they could have done something more to prevent the suicide from occurring; when a student who dies by suicide is a client of a mental health professional working in the campus counseling center or health service, this response is all the more complex.

Following a campus crisis such as a student suicide, some institutions schedule critical incident stress debriefing (CISD) sessions for first responders. Although such interventions have been in place for many years, reliving the critical incident as part of the debriefing process might, in fact, compromise the opportunity for first responders to care for themselves. By participating in the CISD process, responders relive the crisis situation and might be traumatized by the circumstances yet again.

Sample Language for a Postsuicide Intervention Protocol Addressing Student Suicide

Figure 7.3 is an excerpt of a crisis response and postsuicide intervention protocol addressing cases of student suicide. The protocol, developed at a

Figure 7.3. Excerpt of a Crisis Response and Postsuicide Intervention Protocol

<u>**Student Death**</u>

In crisis situations, the primary concern is saving human life. Therefore, first render aid and summon medical assistance for injured people at the scene. Please be aware that all deaths are viewed and investigated by the police as potential homicides until determined otherwise.

The death of any student in the campus community can be a stressful event for a wide array of individuals. Until an official determination is made, the labeling of a death as suicide or homicide may complicate the matter all the more for family, friends, and university staff. For this reason, great care and discretion must be employed in such cases.

<u>**Guidelines**</u>

1. Call 911—University Police Department will alert medical personnel as needed. Be prepared to report your exact location.

NOTE: DO NOT DISTURB A DEATH SCENE
Remember that, unless rendering first aid, it is extremely important not to disturb a death scene. Therefore, exit the area immediately. If at all possible, secure the area in question being careful to touch as little as possible. If there is another person with you, one of you should stay at the scene while the other calls the University Police.

2. The University Police will notify:
a) Hometown police, who will inform parents, guardians, or significant others;
b) The Office of the Vice President for Student Affairs for notification of the President and executive staff. When appropriate, the Vice President's Office will also notify the Office of Media and Marketing for dissemination of information to the public.

3. As soon as possible and within 48 hours, the Vice President for Student Affairs will determine the need for additional support and refer to appropriate individuals or agency resources including:
a) The University Health Center and University Counseling Center for medical/psychological concerns;
b) Campus Ministry, who can provide pastoral services to those affected by the death;
c) Offices in the Division of Student Affairs, whose staff members may be able to address specialized issues if the student is a student of color, an international student, or a student with a disability. Such offices may provide assistance regarding both educational and support services for our diverse population;
d) Offices in the Division of Academic Affairs, including: the appropriate academic dean's office (graduate or undergraduate) who will notify the faculty and provide assistance with academic accommodations, and the Educational Opportunities Program for support of their students;
e) The Director of Residential Life, who will notify Quadrangle Coordinators for transmission of information to their respective Quadrangle staff, such as Residence Directors and Resident Assistants. Residence Hall staff will assess the residents' response to the student's death and may request support services through their supervisory channels and/or through their Quadrangle consultants from the University Counseling Center;
f) The Financial Aid Office, who will notify the employer on campus if the student was employed;
g) The Student Accounts Office, to ensure updating and appropriate management of billing records;
h) The Registrar, to update the student information system.

Figure 7.3. *Continued*

NOTE: CONSULT THE NATURAL SUPPORT SYSTEM
Made up of friends, family, mentors, etc., the natural support system is both essential in providing support to its own members, and at the same time, is likely to also be in need of services. Every effort will be made to work with the natural support system to assist its members in supporting each other and in accessing the broad range of University services listed above.

4. The Office of the Vice President for Student Affairs will coordinate support offered to groups affected by the death, such as the student's friends. Outreach services will be provided, as appropriate, by units such as the Department of Residential Life, University Counseling Center, Office of Multicultural Affairs, Disabled Student Services, or Office of International Education Offices, Chapel House, Educational Opportunities Program, and other offices. Outreach services should address the following points:

FOR STUDENTS:
a) Make timely contact with friends of the deceased student;
b) Encourage expression of feelings;
c) Promote peer support among friends of the victim;
d) Encourage campus attendance at a memorial service as appropriate;
e) Avoid glamorization of death;
f) Encourage resumption of routine as soon as possible.

FOR FAMILY:
a) Make appropriate housing arrangements for parents and/or other family members visiting campus;
b) Offer pastoral care;
c) Offer brief psychological counseling as appropriate;
d) Provide assistance in concluding University business, i.e., gathering the student's personal effects. In this, as in all instances, sensitivity to the family's wishes and requests should be paramount.

5. The Office of the Vice President for Student Affairs will work with Campus Ministry staff to coordinate a university-wide memorial service for the deceased student.

6. Letters of condolence will be sent by the following individuals:
a) The President
b) The Vice President for Student Affairs;

7. The Vice President for Student Affairs will designate an ad hoc group to review the circumstances of the death or suicide approximately two weeks after the event. Units who have played a role in crisis intervention/management of the incident will be represented at the meeting. In addition to a review of the interventions used, post-suicide intervention efforts and support strategies will be discussed as well as recommendations for an enhanced response to similar crises.

large public university in the northeastern United States, is part of a more comprehensive document containing response guidelines focusing on a variety of health and safety concerns.

Summary

A student suicide is a tragic event that can leave an imprint on a college or university and its members for years. Postsuicide intervention protocols that drive a coordinated response to suicide offer a road map to follow in the days after a tragedy, particularly in cases of student suicide, and can offer guidance as campus communities heal and move forward. A comprehensive, clearly written, responsive, and well-executed postsuicide intervention protocol can strengthen a college or university's collective response capacity and forge a path to the best possible outcome when institutions are faced with student suicides and other serious threats to health and safety. Such protocols offer models for collaboration and coordination that assist in addressing emergent concerns and informing future interventions.

Resources

American Foundation for Suicide Prevention. "Reporting on a Suicide: Recommendations for the Media." www.afsp.org/index.cfm?fuseaction=home.viewpage&page_id=7852EBBC-9FB2-6691-54125A1AD4221E49

American Foundation for Suicide Prevention. "Survivor Outreach Program." www.afsp.org/index.cfm?page_id=45225B03-FBF2-AEBB-C260FDE7B93D1BCF

Centers for Disease Control and Prevention. "Recommendations for a Community Plan for the Prevention and Containment of Suicide Clusters." http://wonder.cdc.gov/wonder/prevguid/p0000214/p0000214.asp

Center for Suicide Prevention. "School Memorials After a Suicide: Helpful or Harmful?" www.suicideinfo.ca/csp/assets/alert54.pdf

Clinician Survivor Task Force. "Clinicians as Survivors: After a Suicide Loss." http://mypage.iusb.edu/~jmcintos/therapists_mainpg.htm

Harvard School of Public Health. "Means Matter." www.hsph.harvard.edu/means-matter/

Jed Foundation. "Framework for Developing Institutional Protocols for the Acutely Distressed Student." www.jedfoundation.org/professionals/programs-and-research/framework

Maine Youth Suicide Prevention Program. "Media Guidelines for School Administrators Who May Interact with Reporters about Youth Suicide." www.maine.gov/suicide/professionals/program/mediaschool.htm

Maine Youth Suicide Prevention Program. "Youth Suicide Prevention, Intervention & Postvention Guidelines: A Resource for School Personnel." www.maine.gov/suicide/docs/Guidelines%2010-2009–w%20discl.pdf

National Suicide Prevention Lifeline. "How to Report Suicidal Users on Facebook." www.suicidepreventionlifeline.org/App_Files/Media/PDF/How%20to%20Report%20Suicidal%20Users%20on%20Facebook.pdf

National Suicide Prevention Lifeline. "Lifeline Online Postvention Manual." www.sprc.org/library/LifelineOnlinePostventionManual.pdf

SPAN USA and Suicide Prevention Resource Center. "Guide to Engaging the Media in Suicide Prevention. www.sprc.org/library/media_guide.pdf

Spencer-Thomas, Sally. "When Tragedy Strikes: Suicide Postvention on a College Campus." http://bereavedbysuicide.com/articles/postvention-programs/when-tragedy-strikes-suicide-postvention-on-a-college-campus/

Suicide Prevention Resource Center. "After a Suicide: Recommendations for Religious Services & Memorial Observances." www.sprc.org/library/aftersuicide.pdf

Suicide Prevention Resource Center. "At-a-Glance: Safe Reporting on Suicide." www.sprc.org/library/at_a_glance.pdf

Suicide Prevention Resource Center. "Safe and Effective Messaging for Suicide Prevention." www.sprc.org/library/SafeMessagingfinal.pdf

University at Albany. "Crisis Protocol and Postvention Materials." www.albany.edu/studentaffairs/faculty/albany_only

References

Cerel, J., and Campbell, F. "Suicide Survivors Seeking Mental Health Services: A Preliminary Examination of the Role of an Active Postvention Model." *Suicide and Life Threatening Behavior*, 2008, *38*(1), 30–34.

Drum, D. J., Brownson, C., Burton Denmark, A., and Smith, S. E. "New Data on the Nature of Suicidal Crises in College Students: Shifting the Paradigm." *Professional Psychology: Research and Practice*, 2009, *40*, 213–222.

Garlow, S. J., and others. "Depression, Desperation, and Suicidal Ideation in College Students: Results from the American Foundation for Suicide Prevention College Screening Project at Emory University." *Depression and Anxiety*, 2008, *25*, 482–488.

Haas, A., and others. "An Interactive Web-Based Method of Outreach to College Students at Risk for Suicide." *Journal of American College Health*, 2008, *57*, 15–22.

Meilman, P. W., and Hall, T. M. "Aftermath of Tragic Events: The Development and Use Of Community Support Meetings on a University Campus." *Journal of American College Health*, 2006, *54*(6), 382–384.

National Institute on Alcohol Abuse and Alcoholism. *A Call to Action: Changing the Culture of Drinking at U.S. Colleges.* NIH Pub. No. 02–5010. Bethesda, MD: NIAAA, 2002.

National Suicide Prevention Lifeline. *Lifeline Online Postvention Manual*, 2010. Retrieved January 3, 2012, from www.sprc.org/library/LifelineOnlinePostventionManual.pdf

Suicide Prevention Resource Center. *School Health and Mental Health Care Providers*, 2008. Retrieved December 22, 2011, from www.sprc.org/featured_resources /customized/pdf/school_mentalhealth.pdf

M. DOLORES CIMINI, *PhD, is assistant director for prevention and program evaluation, University Counseling Center, University at Albany, State University of New York.*

ESTELA M. RIVERO, *PhD, is director of the University Counseling Center, University at Albany, State University of New York.*

NEW DIRECTIONS FOR STUDENT SERVICES • DOI: 10.1002/ss

INDEX